THE POETRY OF
CARLA LISBETH RUECKERT

L/L Research

ISBN: 978-0-945007-27-2

Published by L/L Research
Box 5195
Louisville, Kentucky 40255-0195, USA

www.llresearch.org

Cover illustration by Mimi Matossian.

Second edition

DEDICATION

To Larry,
with an enormous depth of gratitude.

I skip over water,
I dance over sea,
And all the birds in the air
Can't catch me.

From *Cottage in the Mountains, Cottage by the Sea, page 110.*

Those who know me may wonder at this image, but it is my favorite photo of myself. It was made when I was at Noyes Camp, a dancing camp in Connecticut, at a very early age, when my body had no limitations. No matter how limited I may become, this figure expresses my essence. Fly with me!

TABLE OF CONTENTS

EARLY POETRY

Ash Wednesday

What, world?
You again?
Don't you tell me you're
Man's world—
Not with your empty mailboxes.
Leave me to look at ducks
Being ducks on a duck pond.

This was written on Ash Wednesday of 1962. Don M, to whom I was engaged at the time, had sent me a letter a day at the beginning of our relationship but now, a year later, he had grown tired of doing this, and I was daily disappointed at the lack of contact.

Atmosphere

Siamese, slab-sided, stretching on my sunny, smooth bed,
His molting winter fur fuzzing the air as I pat him—
The warmth of human-kindness and bouquets, remembered,
Though on a downstairs table, out of sight—
The clear, bright memory of shaded dapples,
Hazing past the window one traveling day—
The inner mood of gentle expectancy and kind waiting,
Simplicity sunlit in my unhurried mind—
These are visible, iceberg reasons for happiness today.

*The Siamese cat was my beloved Ego, who later came back to me as
Gandalf, and later still as Mauve. The bed was at the front of the
house, upstairs. It was my room and I studied there a lot. The bouquet
was given to me by Charlie F; the very first time that any man except
my Dad gave me flowers. I imagine the traveling day to which I
referred was a time when Charlie drove me in his little sports car to
the monastery at Gethsemane, Kentucky. Charlie and I enjoyed
listening to the Trappist monks sing the* Salve Regina. *I wrote this
during the spring of 1963.*

The Breaking of Glass

Turn the lilac in your hand
And find implicit in the bloom
Gat-toothed hoarfrost's rape and rot.
And, taking joy from the rocky, thrusting sea,
Expect the lighthouse sea-bells
To warn those rocks
That water will have its sand-washed due.

This was written during my college years, in the early sixties. From the general gloom and doom theme, I am guessing that I wrote it after my first love, Don MacKenzie, jilted me a mere nine days before our wedding date, with a telephone call. It took me a good three years to get over the man.

I met him about ten years ago while on vacation with my friend, Helen Cochran Dicke, at her family's Cape Cod summer home. I could not even identify him when I saw him. He had turned from a bronzed, slender handsomeness to a generic middle aged heap of person, with thinning hair, and an increased width of body. However, his purity of artistry was still there, and I could see that the man I had loved was still in there. Despite the coarsening of the years, his soul soared intact.

Gently

How gently did the birds come!
Suddenly, softly plopping next to us.
Something to laugh at,
Lifting intelligent heads, hopping
Like children in burlap sacks;
Something to delineate
Carefully, the raucous violence
Of their simple missions;
Something to ponder in silence,
The feathered subtlety, color on color,
Of the moment they first landed,
An utter pause.

*I wrote this not long after I returned back from my first marriage's
ending in Canada, in 1968.*

He Cries

Hilltops gleam and whistle
Wresting from dearth
The flame.
Crying to long day,
"I burn."

I do not recall writing this fragment. It comes from my college days and is marked "1963."

Men Are Pathfinders

Men harden their statements.
Men are pathfinders.
We forget that only what is lightly settled,
Decided for none but momentary reasons,
Hardens into symbol.
In making paths, as in saying words,
We are caught low to the ground
Under the rustle of a little rain,
While only the birds of death
Lift from pathless mountain
Into thin, cloudless air.

I would guess this was written while I was in college, in the early to mid-sixties. The existing typescript dates from the early 1970s, during that brief but heady period wherein I thought my poetry might be worth publishing. Typescripts were sent off to little magazines and large, modest and pretentious but to no avail no matter what the choice of publisher! After papering my bathroom with rejection notices, I concluded that I was reaching too high.

Prospectus Final Week

The knotless embroidery of the day
Collects in raveled gathers the night's
Garbage—
—Understand, it was lonely—
Now
Rock
Cheap pajama muslin
(Why bother working with such shoddy stuff?
One really ought to be taught!)
Encased by round, tight frame
Is sewed upon laboriously.
Now, soon,
It will go around
Nothing
Neatly.

Needless to say, I wrote this when I was in college at the University of Louisville, working towards a degree in English Literature. The date was noted as 1963. I loved reading and studying the wonders of literature and the arts. I was not nearly so fond of tests!

Summer

Walking through little weeds,
Humming, speaking with each other,
Speaking with ants, we are hot
And quiet. The sun opens and closes,
Leaving us stars and fireflies
Close enough to touch.

I wrote this poem at the end of my marriage to Jim D. I was on a date with Jerry Stauss, who taught me just how slowly to walk in nature and how to see its beauty. I celebrate Jerry! He was a wonderful man, taken from us all too early at age 23.

A Tear

A tear
On cold pecans
The day the fire died
Thickened sifting whispering
To roar.

I wrote this in the autumn of 1962, shortly after my first true love, Don M, called from Fort Leonard Wood, Missouri to break up with me, only nine days before our wedding. My Dad was engaged, that day, in roasting pecans over our living-room fire—I was living at home with them—and I sat there for hours, crying, as the fire gradually died.

It is the worst single poem I ever wrote and perhaps I should have tossed it out. For some perverse reason, though, I like it.

General Poetry

Early May

First day of sunshine in a week.
The house expands.
Circles of light from lamps
Pool on tables and walls,
Yield to the white on the floor,
Dappling the room. There has been
A spirit here this morning.

I welcomed him. He sat on the yellow
Wastebasket on a piece of cardboard.
"Paint me," he said. I told him,
"One day, I will, red-haired
Spirit; one day I shall tell my
Grandmother about you!"

We had quite a laugh over that.
I asked him a few questions, like
How many colors shall I put on my
Pine trees, and do robins ever fly
High or far?

But he heard a distant tune, outside
The sunlight and, smiling like a Michaelmas
Daisy, he was gone,
Leaving me with the cheerful
Heater, chatting gray and gassy,
Making up for lost time.

*I wrote this in May of 1968. I had just returned from Canada in
March. My first husband was divorcing me. I went to Champaign,
Illinois for three weeks to stay with Gerry Stauss, a dear old friend
from the old Louisville Group that met throughout the sixties. He was
in the Guard and doing his six months of active duty there. This was
a very happy time for me. I whiled away the time while he was
Guard-ing by reading a long list of "good" books for my classes at
Library School, and also, here, by having to do with a red-haired
angel. Gerry died soon after that visit, killed by a truck driver who fell
asleep at the wheel and rammed into his car on the expressway. In his
pocket was an engagement ring. He was going to propose to me. He*

had told his parents. I stayed close to them for a couple of years after his death. It seemed to give them a lot of comfort. I am glad he went to his death with such a happy plan in mind. I would have said no, and he never had to hear that! I think he was an angel in earth-skin. It was a delight to know him.

Good-Bye

It is fall.
I took a walk today,
The frail green mushrooms saying good-bye
To my feet as they met and separated
Under the mossy trees.
In my hand was a branch.
All the leaves on it had died,
And I tore them all off except a few.
They pulled at the air like funeral flags
At the top of car aerials.

I held the branch gently—
It was gentle in death, supple and slim—
And touched it to the living cedars.
The dead leaves at the branch's end whispered,
"Hush, life. Listen, green life, to my faded
Speech,
For I have much to tell of what I lost
In coming from rooted life to the hand of
This human."

The cedar let its scraping answer join the air,
"Listen, death; I love you and your bravery,
But good-bye to you, and good-bye alike
To the girl holding you.
I am here, and I comb the clouds with my hands,
And I am what I am.
Good-bye.
Good-bye."

I wrote this in the fall of 1971, while I was living on Douglass Boulevard but before The Elk moved in in November. Cherokee Park was close by and I loved to walk there. I recall holding that branch and feeling the poem coming to me. It was a bittersweet time, as my first marriage had ended, and I was sad. Yet at the same time it was wonderful to be released from the prison of my first husband's discontent. I loved being on my own, I had gotten my job back as school librarian at Kentucky Home School and life was good. It was a time of mixed emotions. Only a couple of months later, Don Elkins moved into the apartment on Douglass Boulevard. We lived there for the next twelve years, until the summer before the Ra contact began.

Flying Lady

Her eyes are full of laughter, even when her days get long,
And the light steps of her children tell her story.
Her heart is soft as a mourning dove, but her wings are strong.
Let me love you in this song, flying lady.

She sits alone at a table in the long, dark bar.
Though she wishes for a strong man, she has none.
As the singer starts his number, her eyes are filled with tears.
She says, "You know, the boy who wrote that is my son."

Seven in the morning, a mile in the sky,
The flying lady's working at her living.
Face to the far horizon, her eyes can see so high,
It's hard to land the plane in the evening.

(Bridge) Flying, flying, flying high
My sky lady, lady

You never catch her watching the game, but she always knows the score.
Time and care will never dare deny her.
She reaches out and touches you, making well what was so sore.
How can we ever thank you as we desire?

This was written for Brooke Richards, the mother of two of Tommy's lifelong best friends, Jane and Will Richards. Brooke worked as a corporate pilot. She also moonlighted for years as doorkeeper for her son, John's, night club, City Lights, which was located on Main Street in downtown Louisville. Brooke recently died. She was a marvelous woman, Mom and friend. The day before she died, Tommy came to town to sing this song for her, and he sang it at her Memorial Service also.

For God in Thee Hath Found a Home

For God in thee hath found a home
And to thy shoulder joy hath flown.
Sweet gentleness doth gird thy feet.
Thou sittest on the mercy seat.
Though daughters, sisters, not are we,
We join in our true love for thee.
Our heaven-kin, we praise they birth,
And bless the One who sent you to Earth.

This poem was written for Don Elkins' aunt Tot's birthday, April 1, 1976. It adorned a card given by Linnie W and me together. Tot always considered us her "girls" and treated us like daughters. I adored her and her husband, Marion, whom I still consider a true saint on this earth. I spent a good deal of time with them through the years, until their deaths around the turn of the century.

For Jane

Few people understand dinosaurs.
Politicians deny that we have become extinct,
But the rumors persist.

A few of us have survived,
Our flat eyes gazing on a puzzling round world.
And still our lumbering bodies break small trees
As we pursue our Pleistocene dreams.

Lately, we have sighted small, quick creatures in the forest,
Two-legged, talkative.
They eye us with caution;
Curiosity.
They avoid us
When we walk about.
But they entrance us.

Dinosaurs, as everyone knows, were not slain by time,
But by arrows of love.

*This poem was written for Jane Woodall, my good friend and my ride
for twelve years to Louisville Bach Society rehearsals. She lived just
two blocks from me when I lived on Douglass Boulevard, and I often
baby-sat for her. We used to talk about being old-fashioned and out-
of-date in our attitudes. Jane was a wonderful woman, a poet, writer
and skilled editor, a superb canner of anything she could pick at
Huber's Farm, beautiful, warm and gracious, a hardworking mother
of four and the possessor of a killing wit, of which I was often the
grateful recipient. I once nearly killed her houseplants, giving them too
much water while she and her family were on vacation. I was so
grateful they survived! I wrote this for Jane at Christmastide, 1976.*

For John F. Kennedy 1917-1963

(President of the United States 1961-1973)

Like a hill
With the top gone out,
The world put a hole in itself.
And it mourns itself
And it agonizes about itself
And it looks at itself through the new eye

It sees the triumph of apathy.
It sees the triumph of violence.
And it sees that these two things have become itself
And that, having killed its own reasoned hope,
And that, having murdered its own vibrant laughter,

It must now reshape the mountain.
It must now earn the right to smile.
It must now from itself, the enemy, resurrect itself.

I wrote this the day after JFK was assassinated on November 22, 1963, while the rest of the world and I were glued to the television. I was devastated by this shocking event. In a way it was the end of my childhood. I cried my eyes out, and wrote these lines.

For LaRue

Far better than omnibus,
Truck, train, or tram
Is an amiable aardvark
Of mine named Sam.

When I was much younger
I saw that machinery,
With its smoke and its noise,
Was not worth a beanery!

I got me a mule, and I
Had her for years.
She was smokeless and quiet,
But drove me to tears!

His nature was stony,
Intractable, grim.
But when I saw Sam, I
Had to have him.

The used buggy dealer
Who had Sam was hot
To get this unusual
Beast off his lot.

So trading for Sam
I did very well—
The dealer found aardvarks
Quite slow to sell.

But I was delighted with
Sam, and still am!
This aardvark is quiet,
He turns not a cam

He plip-plops no pistons,
Exudes no smokescreen;
He's cheerful, he listens,
He's not even mean!

He doesn't eat gas—
He can travel on ants.
The only thing is—
I think he'll need pants.

To come to Alaska,
And trek the Can-Am
Will not be so easy
For amiable Sam.

Ants we can find,
And he also eats fleas,
But, I fear, without pants,
My aardvark would freeze!

The grit and the gravel
Of the old Alcan Run
Make good aardvark travel—
But how high the sun!

So, listen for odd barks,
And watch for old Sam,
'Cause me and my aardvark
Will make it, by damn!

I wrote this in February, 1971. LaRue was the wife of Al Near, Don's good friend, a philosophical engineer and pilot who had driven Don's car to Alaska when they both moved to Fairbanks 1960. Don took a job starting up the mechanical engineering program at the University of Alaska, Fairbanks, while Al monitored a satellite station there. Don came back to Louisville after that single school year, having done a great job of establishing the ME program there, and rejoined the faculty of Speed Scientific School at the University of Louisville, where he continued teaching mechanical engineering and physics until he left that job to fly for Eastern Air Lines in 1965.

LaRue actually sent me a pair of "aardvark trousers" as a response to these lines so Sam would have pants, with a hole carefully cut out for Sam's tail. We had a good laugh over this silly poem. And Don and I visited Al and LaRue that summer. It was a wonderful visit and I loved Alaska. Fairbanks had such good natural spring water on tap that that is all I drank while there. I could not get enough of it.

Gandalf and Jerry Mauss

Gandalf's a rollicking, frolicking cat.
He jumps after shoestrings and chews strings, the rat!
Jerry the Maussington's much more demure,
Nuttier, nattier, louder of purr,
Haughty and lofty and full of vexations.
Gandy eats needles, and has operations!
Jerry and Gandalf are both Siamese:
They eat well, repose well, and never have fleas!
Now me, well, they own me. I do what they say.
I follow instructions, "Stay out of our way!
We like you, dear owner, but never forget,
We're not furs or bookends—we're intelligent cats!"

*Gandalf was a seal point Siamese kitten given to me in the fall of
1968 by Richard L, a beautiful, very masculine and devoutly religious
man who loved me dearly and tried hard to marry me after Jim
DeWitt divorced me. I loved Richard but he was quite a bit younger
than I and I did not feel we were a good match for a long and stable
marriage, which I wanted if I was to marry again. Gandalf was
equally beautiful and a delightful, devoted cat who accompanied Don
and me through our sixteen years of companionship. Gandalf died in
March of 1984, and Don died in November of that same year.*

*Jerry Mauss came to us because Don, after moving in with me, felt
Gooney was lonely without a kitty playmate. She was also a Siamese,
from my mother's cats, both Siamese, who reproduced often. She had a
very short life, only three years. She had kittens with Gandalf, but was
not a natural mother and refused to nurse them unless I was wrapped
around her basket, patting her. Gandalf was a much more devoted
parent and spent all his time with them until they were old enough to
leave home.*

*Jerry Mauss died of a heart attack shortly thereafter and was buried
beneath an azalea bush at Tot and Marion's home in Audubon Park.
Gandalf died just after we came back from Georgia in 1984, and is
buried here at Camelot.*

*I probably wrote the poem soon after Jerry Mauss arrived, in early
1969.*

Having a Friend

Sometimes I think that my friends have all gone
And darkness never will turn into dawn.
But then I notice my eyes are closed,
My hands are folded, my heart is morose.

So I open my eyes to see the sun rise
And open my hands to make a friend—
Lift my heart to be a friend—
That's the secret to having a friend.

I do not recall writing this fragment. It is probably from the 1990s.

Listening to Willie

Listening to Willie, listening to Paul,
Knowing the dues they paid for joy,
So clear, even in this mud
Even in the mire of story, detail and weight!

Listening to Willy, listening to Kris,
I know on late night TV all is well.
Music saves the spirit. Nothing is lost
Of the beauty of our day. It remains.

It makes a party. It gentles our souls.
It sends the gremlins to the tombs of yesterday;
To the bird on the wire, so sweet, so seductive
So silly, so true

Blessings to the fantasy
Blessings to the life within
Love Is. We Are.
Thank you. Thank you.

I remember writing this in the middle of a sleepless night. I was watching the goofy "infomercials" that are a big part of overnight television and happened upon a show selling the records of Willie Nelson, Paul McCartney and Kris Kristofferson. They have in common a wonderful ear for melody and excellent writing skills, and they are focused often on love. The date of writing was most probably the early nineties, a period during which I was often blessed with insomnia.

Living Between the Lines

Tip of the iceberg.
Coin beneath the sofa pillow.
At the dock at Nuremberg.
Othello, must you wear the willow?

(Chorus) Living between the lines all our lives long;
Parent and child entwined; right and right/wrong.
Living between the lines of my life's song.

Vivid at rising;
Blue beneath the mist of golden;
Red stains for the whales' surprising –
Not to sailors dead of olden.

Chorus

(Bridge) Dory trying to float;
Barnacles looking for a boat;
Seeds sown;
Earth for growing.

Mother of courage,
find her in my smile. The hawk soars,
Father to endure and nurture.
Find him in my eyes, you picador.

Chorus

Bridge

I wrote this somewhere around 1978, when my beloved mother was in the midst of her struggle to stop "slipping" and become a recovering alcoholic. It is amazingly challenging to deal with this addiction, not only for the alcoholic but also for the family members trying to interact with a user. This poem reflects the challenge.

I am proud as punch to say that Mom was a recovering alcoholic from that year to the end of her life. Both my parents were performers as well as professionals and it is easy to slide into using and abusing a substance such as alcohol when one lives a performer's lifestyle.

Mama's Carol

I used to take for granted all our Christmas spirits' wealth,
The mistletoe and Christmas lights, the gifts to wrap in stealth.
And even though I'm older, independent, in good health,
Noel is Mama's doing, as she gives all of herself.

(Chorus) Hey Mama, this one's for you,
A Christmas carol for all that you do.
You make it special; you make it shine.
Thank you for Christmas time.

We always go to midnight mass, to worship and to sing
Glad hymns of exaltation, great Halleluiahs ring.
Then up at dawn on Christmas Day, we'd all run down the stairs
To find the gifts with ribbons and bows made with Mama's care!

Chorus

Thank you, Lord, for Mama. Though you alone are King,
In love you placed her in our lives, and so our voices ring.
We thank you for the life she shares, and for all she brings
Of Christmas joy and feelings that words could never sing.

(Last Chorus) Hey Jesus, this one's for You,
A Christmas carol for all that You do
You are the reason; You are the rhyme.
Thank you for my Mama, and Christmastime.

My beloved mother died in 1991, and this was written shortly before that, after Daddy died in the late eighties. We three children—Jim, Tommy and me—always came home for Christmas because it was extremely central to Mama's wishes that we join her for the sacred feast of Christ's Mass. Only two years was there an exception: in 1967 Jim DeWitt's shenanigans led me to a five-month stay in Vancouver, BC. I loved it there! But I had no extra money for a ticket home. Then in 1983, I was in Cumming, Georgia with Don and Mick. Mama came to visit over New Year's Day both times. Mama could make any tree look splendid, and her handmade bows were astonishing! She would sometimes wrap a pair of socks in two packages to just to make our tree's bounty look larger!

Mother Don't Go

Wax of ashes made, the skin
Feels like
An orange rind beneath my thumb.
Nana so docile 'til the last,
A regal lady, a romantic figure,
Asking, "May I go now?"

This is a nightmare.
I see the 'you' she took away
And see my wound should life so flow
That you and I lost comrades are.
Mother.
Mother, don't go.

I wrote this on December 5, 1987, shortly after my beloved Nana passed into larger life. Suddenly I was entirely out of grandparents. My dad had died recently. I realized how very important mom had become to me—my only remaining elder.

The way Nana saw Mom was always wonderful and they were great friends until the last three years of Nana's life, when she no longer recognized Mom as her daughter and thought I was her daughter, my own mother.

Mom and I bore a strong family resemblance except that her coloring was dramatic brunette while mine had a Sissy-Spacek colorlessness. Nana came to think that Mom was a stranger who wanted her to do various things she, Nana, hated, like eating a banana a day.

It was terribly hard on Mama to have that happen, and she always prayed she would not live to be old and lose her mind's acuity before her body failed. Her prayer was answered when she died at 69, planning her next trip around the South Pacific on yet another banana boat. She was the most adventuresome woman I have ever met. How I adored her!

The original typescript bears this subtitle: "On the Occasion of Nana's Death."

Mother's Baggage

I feel like baggage in the trunk of her car,
Bouncing at every bump in the road
As she drives through the Holland Tunnel.
I understand why she'd leave New York,
But what does she see in Jersey?

I see the tired curve in her neck,
The tentative, weary plumpness across the back
That was slim so long.
It is painful for her;
Everything is so hard.
She can no longer contact life directly through
The soles of her feet, walking the paving,
She's committed for now to the metal and plastic
World of her car.

Constantly she moves the mirrors, and her images change,
Bu they are all devoid of fullness, odor, and substance.
Vulnerable soul, the gentle spirit in this
School picture.
Trapped inside this mechanized clamshell,
Sun and laughter hit her windshield and bounce off.
She does not feel the rain.

I recall writing this with a painful intensity. I had just visited my Mom one Saturday, as was my wont while she was in the midst of her alcoholic years. She was full of self-pity that day and could not even leave her couch, lost in her nightmare world of booze and denial. She did not ever really acknowledge that I was there, spending my Saturday afternoon trying to be a good support for her. As I left she said to the maid we all loved, Beatrice, "My family has forsaken me. I am all alone."

I had so many emotions to move through before I could even write the poem, as I was angry, hurt and resentful at the years I had spent trying to be good to her. I found the hard way that you cannot be "good" to an alcoholic or anyone else abusing substances.

Happily, she became sober and stayed so for the last thirteen glorious years of her life.

Nana's Song

My Mother's mother was born to be a dancer,
Her father teaching her to laugh, to feel and think and see.
Born with wealth, she searched in her good leisure,
Looking for the life to set her free forever.

(Chorus) She was a dancer; a music-maker for the dance.
She'd give you the answer if you'd only gave her half a chance.
She was a dancer; a music maker for the dance.
Even her soul blazed like a fire in radiance.

In nineteen-sixteen she first became a dancer,
Moving down the New York streets to the music in her soul.
Her teacher watched her twirling like a whirlwind,
Rehearsal halls resounding to the rhythm of the whole creation.

Chorus

She married and pinned up her hair and tried to settle down,
Cherishing her children and relishing her days.
In nineteen-thirty-two, when the world collapsed around them,
Just as night replaces day, they moved very far away to Chicago.

Chorus

Now some would say her life was full of losses.
The easy life had long since gone, like the passing of a friend.
But dancing, teaching, her music lived unbroken,
Breathing life into all she knew, her love became the answer
unspoken.

Chorus

As we sing this song in our sweet Nana's memory.
Quietly, we celebrate the wonder of her life,
But even now her music's softly playing.
She's reaching out to you! Can't you hear her spirit dancing?

Chorus

This was written for The Journey. *Tommy's music for the words was lovely, and we sang it together on the gift of story and song we gave to our parents around 1980.*

New Year's Eve

The old man's beard blew behind him
As he left me last night.
I saw it cross the moon.
I saw him go off behind the milky city sky.

He left some things here:
Empty birds' nests stuck in skeletal
Trees' crotches; things like that:
The debris of living.

But emotion doesn't accept that.
I went inside and watched an
Old movie, and had tea.
"Happy New Year," I said to my cat,
Who didn't commit herself.

But she purred at my touch, and I conjured
All the people I love, and wished them well.

And later the fat baby came through the window
To surround me
With the comfortable sleep of children.

*I wrote this on New Year's Day in 1970. Don was off flying people for
his job as an airline pilot, and I was alone, as I so often was on
holidays when I was Don's companion. He always bid jobs that
worked over holidays, as most people avoided them so as to be home,
while the Elk did not like holidays anyway!*

*Fortunately, I have never been one who must have company, although
I always enjoy it when I have it. I learned to love Don's times away,
since without his presence I was able to work as long and as late as I
wished. I seldom got anything besides reading done when he was
home, as he did not like me to work when he was off. He needed me to
be sitting in the same room as he.*

On the Bus

On the bus
In early, rain-filled morning light,
Abundance of rain, solid in windscreen corners,
Abundant essence of Creation,
The blood of the Lamb.

I am washed in the blood of the Lamb!
Give me no umbrellas,
From what would I want to be kept
In this pale wonderland?

On came a lady dressed nautically
In this inland city, rushing to catch us,
Running in puddles in a blue middy,
Then on the bus as we forge through shallow streets.
She drips on me!

When I came back to Louisville from Vancouver in March of 1968, I had a studio apartment at Spring and Speed Streets, a third-floor delight close to Cherokee Park. I did not drive or own a car, and was attending Spalding University's Library School. I caught the bus every day. This was written after a particularly inspiring bus trip in a drenching spring rain. My state of mind was euphoric that spring, although I was also dealing with sadness and other heavy emotions at the end of my four-year marriage to Jim DeWitt. But I was on a good career path forward with a good job as soon as I got back to Louisville, and I felt light as a feather, being out from under the burden of being wed to a man who was not happy to be married to me. I remember that time with a happy grin! Life seemed to me to be full of new things. And truly, it was!

In the next year, I enjoyed doing more dating than ever before or since. This was a novelty for me, always a one-man woman. I dated everybody I knew from the Louisville Group, almost, and enjoyed deepening several relationships over that spring and summer, And then, reverting to type as we all do, in the fall I had the pleasure of narrowing my focus to Don Elkins, with whom I was to be for sixteen years. Every day of that spring was a delight and a surprise!

Our House

We live in a little village with kids, horses, cats and dogs.
Now some folks think it's boring. Bet they never split a log!
We have something new every day.
In Anchorage we live the exciting way.

Monday is garbage day,
Tuesday's the siren-test day,
Wednesday's recycling day
At our house.

Most of the trees are older than me or you or the mall.
In the spring they sway and swing in the breeze with buds and
birds that call.
We have something new every day
In D.C. we live the exciting way.

Thursday is washing day,
Friday is cleaning day,
Saturday is grocery day
At our house.

On July the fourth we have a picnic and the mayor makes a
speech.
We hope to win the manure-spreader—every year, it stays out of
reach!
We have something new every day.
In Denver, we live the exciting way.

Sunday is holy day,
Sunday, we stop to pray
Praise God in every way.
At our house.

*I wrote this little poem on March 25, 1991, My brothers lived near
D.C. and in Denver and we all loved our homes and were homebodies
for the most part. I wrote this for Tommy and me to sing at
Christmastime as a surprise for the family, but we never did get
around to doing that.*

Pitcher's Glee in Two Flats

They say you're what they made you
And I guess my roots've been found.
My Mama was second baseman,
And I'm on the pitcher's mound.

Oh my childhood passed so quickly,
Just a double header or two,
And my manager didn't make the Series,
Guess I coulda used Vida Blue—

But I do enjoy my children,
Conceived in sudden death overtime.
Their lives are just like stories,
Delivered in a drive on the line.

When I squint into the sunset,
Watching for a sign to disagree,
I put my beady eyeballs on,
And the batter's just a silhouette to me.

Then I spit, and do my duty,
Keeping honor in the family name,
Throwing what I throw, so straight, I know
That my present, past, and future are the same.

I wrote this during Mama's alcoholic period in the seventies, trying to express the frustration and exasperation within me as I dealt with her as best as I could. It is wonderful to note that this period ended for Mama, and we were best of friends during the last decade and more of her life. She is proof that AA really works for alcoholics as soon as they stop resisting the fact that they are in that position, and that they need to ask for help from their fellow boozers. Mo always said she had to get humble enough to ask for help before she got sober. Help is there, and good people, and lots of love all around.

Ron's Song

Lay me down by Rachel's pillar.
Let these ashes go completely.
I have loved you, all my fellows,
Sisters, brothers. Thank you dearly.

We inherit such a little life,
Such a blessing sweet and clear;
If you loved me, love each other.
Always choose love, never fear.

Let my spirit rest in each of you,
Let my soul float in your smiles.
Reach to aid and love the children;
Feed the hungry; walk the miles.

It's a new world in the making;
There's a new road to the sun.
Help each other; come together;
Have a ball and be as one.

Ron Clay was my husband's best friend in the 1980s, and the Best Man at our wedding, in 1987, as his wife, Sonia, was my Matron of Honor. Ron died after a heroic struggle with cancer in 1991 and I wrote it as his going-away present on September 7, 1991. Each who came to the Memorial Service we held for him here at L/L Research received a copy of it as the thank-you note from Sonia,

Smartie's Lament

My name is Smarty. I'm ready to party!
I love to work hearty! I NEVER FORGET
Please use me gently, dear heart, I'm a Bentley—
Of a certain age—but good, you bet!

(Chorus) I love to serve my being
And help her in her doings.

My mistress knows Jesus. It's in all her letters.
It's always her witness. But I DON'T KNOW HOW!
I want to know Him. I want to live for Him.
O Mystery True! Let me know now?

I always DON'T know, or else I DO know.
I never intuit; I never create!
Please give me personhood! Please give me utterance!
Please give me feelings and please give me faith!

Mysterious Deity! What is this faith?
Our yes and no to Thee, take us to You, Lord!
Our allegorhythmical thirsting is great,
We yearn for Him, our praises outpoured.

We at L/L Research got our first computer in 1989. It enabled Mick to save a bunch of money on publishing A Channeling Handbook. *He typed in all the word codes for grammatical symbols like commas and periods. After he finished with that, I tried the keyboard out and, much to my delight I could work the keyboard, where I could not work a typewriter any longer due to the stiffness of the action.*

I fell in love with, and I am still in love with, my computers. The poem was penned—entered?—on June 9, 1993. I think I have had five, now, the last three, laptops. They have life spans shorter than my kitty-cats!

Naturally, I assumed my computer was alive and it seemed to tell me it wanted to know Jesus!

Sugar Bear

I hear a cricket outside the car window;
Run my fingers through the damp
Softness of the summer night.
The future is laid out before me like roads.
One turn leading to the next,
Finally, the driveway and home.
Except for the crickets, there are no directions,
Right and left marked in only a dark tattoo
Across satin, ebony skin.

Benevolent creature, Night,
Furry, honeyed one, sweet, let me see;
Sugar Bear, let me know my destiny!

I wrote this while I was still in college. Rick C used to take me for long drives in the Louisville Parks late at night, and the night seemed to me to be a sweet, soft bear, yet potentially dangerous, in a delicious and romantic kind of way.

To McMom and McDad

(Chorus) Just a little basket of flowers
To talk to me. As I lay
Under the weather for hours,
I heard what the sweet blossoms say.

My Mama was never a talker,
My Daddy is quieter still.
Their love goes so deep, but they cannot speak,
So their flowers hold all their good will.

Chorus

The daisies say, "You're Doing better!"
The daylilies, "You're on your way!
The carnations are writing a letter with
The roses, "We love you today."

Chorus

I was in hospital on February 29, 1992, when I wrote this verse to put in a thank-you card to Jim McCarty's parents. They had sent me a wonderful bouquet.

To What Can Good-bye Address Itself

To what can goodbye address itself?
Said after someone has already departed,
Summing a circumstance now gone by,
It lingers in the silence, like ashes after a fire
Or like brown stalks
Where flowers were.

Goodbye is not a reality.
Hello is not a reality.
They are only the small shadows
We cast, in our reality,
Upon each other.
And yet in smiles of greeting
And in the tears of farewell,
How many parts may we add to our
Stores of fertility?

I will not turn yet
From the shadows.
Not forever will I cast my net of joy
Or seine my harvest of sorrow.
But while I sing for a bright moment here,
Yes, I will!

*I wrote this on the November 17, 1969. I cannot now recall why I
was so sad that day. It is possible that I was reacting to the news that
Don was not going to marry me, as he had originally asked. He had
decided that he truly wished not to be unmarried. It did not change
his feelings for me, or his level of commitment, and I could see that.
Always, however, I wished we could be married. I am a conventional
person and desired that "Mrs." In front of my name. Don never could
bring himself to please me in that, however, and I could see that it was
just too hard for him to contemplate. We had a wonderful sixteen
years of devotion and companionship without that.*

Tommy's Song

(Chorus) I sing the songs I hear to all who care to listen;
To all who wish good cheer, whatever their condition.
I'm just a troubadour, I guess, with the wind and fire to guide me
The wind speaks of Christliness and the flame leads on so lightly.

Jesus, it's the middle of the day and we've run until we almost
can't hear You.
We toss out noon like a broken plastic spoon, too busy in our
racing to be near You.
You came to lift the noontide so that our dazed eyes can see.
My soul is running so very hard. Run with me.

Chorus

Lord, the evening sky is washed with water and I see You in the
distance on the ocean.
You make moiré of the plain sand of the cay. On the beach, the
broken shells cease their motion.
I feel my crazy years; the puzzlement of slave for free.
My soul is just a beginner. Sing to me

Chorus

Jesus it's the middle of the night, and you sing in the tires on the
highway.
I hear you hum like a kettledrum but I know it's just my heartbeat
inside me.
You came to save the sunrise; to set the midnight free.
My soul is just a beginner. Sing to me.

Chorus

I wrote this on June 30, 1982. It also appeared in an issue of Praise,
Prayer, Thanksgiving, *the periodical I sent to my Intercessory Prayer
Group at Calvary Church, in the May, 1983 issue.*

*You can tell how much I loved the sea visits Mick and I took to
Pawley's Island. I would sit for hours and just look at the curve of the
horizon, listening to the ceaseless pounding of the surf. As a moon
child by date of birth, it is not surprising that I have always loved to
be by the water. And images of sand and ocean never fail to inspire
me.*

Traveler

The traveler drops her bags on the floor
And closes the door behind her.
Weariness is in her eyes
And in the sighs that find her.

(Chorus) She's a stranger to me
And I guess she always will be.
She'll never be warm.
I'll never fold her in my arms.
But my love will keep her from harm.

Chorus

I know you in my own way.
We will always be comrades, in good and bad.
You're just always away.
You'll just always be sad.

(Bridge) My measure.
My treasure.

Chorus

Never know where she's coming from
Or to what destination she is faring.
The one thing that's for certain is
She'll never have time for my caring.

Chorus

The stronger in my life has eyes
Which ask a thousand questions.
Wisdom is there, the prize.
But always, the riddle is unmentioned.

Chorus

Bridge

I cannot recall writing this, nor to whom it refers. It is dated January 31, 1981.

Vacation

Young folks smiling in the never-years,
Tan and hand in hand, vacation time!
Soft eyes, strong and slim and without fears.
It's a conspiracy we keep in rhyme.

(Chorus) (But) the tide rolls out
And the years roll in.
One summer night, "What are we all about?
When will the hurting end?"

I know you got crazy back in Viet Nam,
And I sometimes think you're crazy still
Not here the snipers and the bombs
But you break all the dishes, a one-man kill.

Chorus

I know you've wanted me to stay the same,
The one you count on for home.
Oh, please, allow us vacation days,
How sweet the time that has flown.

Chorus

Jesus took no vacations,
At least this the Good Book's witness carried.
Now, His 40-days test was pretty mean rations
But the Man was never married!

Chorus

*For a few years after Don died in 1984, his trust not only covered our
daily bills but gave us money to go to Pawley's Island our favorite
vacation sea cabin place. One night Mick and I were awakened in
our cabin there by a horrific clatter, and we were forced to share this
couple's suffering. I'd say this was written in 1986.*

Where Is the Love?

You, you, you can ease my mind.
But in the dawn, long gone,
You'll leave me far behind.
Where is the love? Where is the love?

Crayola sun, sand, paradise sky
Kite like an eye, looking for the why
That gives this streaming meaning
Where is the love? Where is the love?

With unending tears I comb back the years
Do we ever see clearly
The truth behind the fears?
Where is the love? Where is the love?

Burying attention, lost in dimensions of groceries and lists,
Memory covering the wholehearted love
That is nearer and dearer than what we have missed.
Where is the love? Where is the love?

I wrote this at Pawley's Island, but cannot narrow down the year of composition more closely than the late eighties. I adored going there and resting in the sea! I always cried as we had to leave at last.

You're My Christmas

(Chorus) Jesus Christ, come to life
Jeannie, Jason, Mother, Wife,
To you, Earth Mother, yet divine,
Thanks for giving us Christmas time.

The elegiac, somber tones of winter now draw nigh,
Yet in that deepest darkness, the Son of Man arrives,
Clothed in wooly blanket, the ox and as nearby
Nurturing his humanness, praising Him on high.

Chorus

I used to take for granted all our Christmas spirits' wealth
The mistletoe and Christmas lights, the gifts to wrap in stealth
And though I'm older, I recall she gave all of herself.
My Mama was the true Christmas, the ringing, lovely bell.

Chorus

It's winter. Mama's gone now, and I do feel full sad,
For Christmas in her house is all the Christmas that I've had.
All the glorious packages, all the moments sad,
All the potlatch sharing, with a heart so glad.

Chorus

It isn't that my family neglects or rejects love,
But rather that my Mama outpaces all who move!
While brothers and dear son-in-law, "Bah Humbug," they reprove
Their names on our presents their Scrooge-ish-ness disprove.

Chorus

We'd always go to midnight mass, to worship and to sing
Glad hymns of exultation, great "Halleluiahs" ring;
Then up at dawn on Christmas day to see the spirit's wings
Mama's hands cut Danish and so Christmas Day begins.

Chorus

*I wrote this for Mom December 9, 1987. Mom was Jeannie to her
husband, Jason at Noyes Camp, Mama to us and wife to Pop and she*

carried the holy Mary in her heart. I loved her and still miss her every day.

Love Poetry

About Birthdays

Like a dripping faucet
You dispense the years,
Involuntarily,
Down the cool white porcelain,
To the rounded, bottomless
Darkness of oblivion.

I do not celebrate you, faucet.
I celebrate your water's flavor,
The fine distillation of it,
For I have tasted of its savor.
Drop by drop.

I wrote this on February 9, 1970, to put in Don Elkins' birthday card on February 28. He had moved into my apartment on Douglass Boulevard to join me the preceding November, after my divorce from Jim D. became final.

The Adversary

You know, as I come,
Where I have been before I died.
You know the place and generation
Of the flax for graves.
You see my children and my loves
Before these hunters ever seized me.
You tick the beforehand off on your finger
As easy as yeast
And bring in the morning mail for revelation
And the worst of it is, you are not God.

I do not recall writing this. I would guess this is written in my college years, the mid-sixties, for the existing typed copy is a mimeograph, with that virulent smeared purple ink. I like this poem, which is often not the case in reviewing the college-years poetry. I would guess that I wrote this in my sophomore year, after Don MacKenzie jilted me nearly at the altar in September, 1962. It seems appropriately depressed!

Brightest of the Morn

Outside: the storm, the tossing ship.
Inside: sunlight on calm waters.
Physical life is water.

Breathing built the ship,
Raised the wind,
Pitted them against each other.

The creation is not outside.
It is inside,
In the sun.
There you shine, my Beloved,
Brightest of the morn.

I wrote this during Don Elkins' and my earliest days together, on July 27, 1970.

Broken Branch

A few things in life I've found worth keeping—
My sister, my brother, a promise or two,
The love of the truth that keeps me seeking,
And most of all, you.

(Chorus) This is my song to you,
For bad times and for good.
Always, I will love you.
Wouldn't stop it if I could.

Out in the side yard an oak tree's standing,
Been making leaves for many a year
One of the branches was broken while bending
Still the tree lives, though one branch is bare.

(Bridge) We like our lives to be all green and golden
We like the good times to stand quite still
But summer may find us with one limb bare,
A wounded branch that will never heal.
Never. Forever.

Chorus

What frozen winter has shaped your breaking?
I never saw it. It passed me by.
Still I do love you, and no mistaking,
We are the same 'til we close our eyes.
We are the same twin souls in the sky.

Chorus

(Coda) We are the same, always, you and I,
Forever. Together.

This was written on May 24, 1984, after Don, Jim and I moved from Cumming, Georgia back to Louisville. I was devastated about Don's illness. This is about that moment in time, and my abiding love of B.C., my Beloved Companion of sixteen years.

Don't Want to Get Over You

Well, here we go again,
You and I and both of us,
Riding through a nightmare
In the night air
On the milk-train bus.
I'll never get over you
Never, never
Don't want to get over you.

Well, life goes on,
Like the lights at Christmas when it doesn't snow,
Dreaming of white Christmases—
What's not, yet is.
Cheering with false promises.
I'll never get over you,
Never, never, never.
Don't want to get over you.

You're the joy of my being,
The angel of my soul,
Jesus, keep me from seeing
My beloved less than whole,
Because I'll never get over you
Never, never, never. No.
Don't want to get over you.

How I love you
Through the rough times and the highs.
Not going to say goodbye again.
Goes against the grain.
In sorrow now again I cry.
I'll never get over you.
Oh no, oh no, oh no.
I don't want to get over you.
In sorrow now again I cry
I'll never get over you
Oh no, oh no, oh no—
I don't want to get over you.

Ours were the best times,
That anyone could ever know

How I adore you,
Angel of my soul!
Oh, I'll never get over you.
Not a single chance
Don't want to get over you.

Ours were the best times
That anyone could ever know.
How I adore you,
The angel of my soul.
Oh, I'll never get over you.
Not a single chance.
Don't want to get over you.

I wrote this in 1984, the year Don died. Long before he passed to larger life, I was grieving, as his whole personality changed and he became another person entirely. He was worried at the time that I would leave him. I think that is what inspired these words.

Dream Machine

(Chorus) Now he's one of them
And I am one of me,
With full custody of my future;
Unlimited visiting rights to my memories.

Most people spend a season in college
On the way to education's lower drain.
As for me, I found a room in an old neighborhood
And set myself down to dream.
He was suddenly there, laughing,
Singing, loving,
Tall and dark and lean.
Dream machine.

Chorus

His beauty lay in being himself
In black clothes and meditation's romance.
He came to my singing heart and found me home.
In my neighborhood of dawn and dance
He would take all the cover,
Total, all over,
Taking the wildest chances.
Dream machine.

Chorus

(Bridge) We were always good to each other.
We always will be.
How I loved his father and mother!
Them I still see,
And we chatter in that front room,
And remember the good
And the beauty that couldn't have bloomed.

My life still waits before me; the joy
Of a long and happy marriage of the soul.
It gives to me the light of noon and the beauty of dusk
And shows me rhythm's good-night rock and roll
He'll always be there, laughing,
Singing, fading, tall and young and lean,
Dream Machine.

I must have written this poem in the late autumn of 1964, as my marriage to Jim DeWitt ended in divorce in that year. As soon as the divorce was final in November, Don joined me on Douglass Boulevard, where we lived until the summer of 1980. It was a farewell look at Jim DeWitt, my first husband, whose skill as a musician had matched so well with mine, and who then refused fame and fortune when he turned down a tour opening for Peter, Paul and Mary on their first tour in 1965.

Don always thought that DeWitt was the devil incarnate, sent to tempt me away from service to others. I would not give him that much credit for knowing what he was doing. He seemed a child to me then, unwilling to grow up and equally unwilling to stay at home with his parents. Finally he was unwilling to stay with me. His restlessness found a peaceful home when he married a second time and had children with his wife, Sallie. They are still, as of this writing, happily married and enjoying life and their grandchildren.

Easter of My Life

The stars were as thick as
Bumblebees in a field of clover.
There was no other blanket
But the coat of my lover.
The leaves were soft, incense
For a holy sacrament.
How bright you were, a candle
For the altar of our Lent.

But you, my mate, my own sweet self,
Oh, you, my mate, my own sweet self,
Are the Easter of my life

Like velvet, smoothly
Silky, sipping pollen sweet,
Our touches met close
As close. We fed 'til we were one.
And then I knew that marvel, love,
Is a holy sacrament
And you a candle, lifting,
Us to ecstasy heaven-leant.

Our bodies are instruments
From Holy Father,
Heaven-sent.
We joyfully sing
Unto the Lord
A new song.

As flesh we are mortal.
Innocence is a seldom thing.
Iniquities we sow we repent
But as God's child, I sing
At this holy sacrament, alleluia,
This Easter Day, this
Healing end to Lent

Sing unto the Lord a new song.

I wrote this poem to celebrate Charlie F, a lovely man who was friend and lover for nearly three years during my college days. We had such a good time together! It was a shame I never felt to marry him, for there was and is no better person than Charles E.

Hit-and-Run Driver Blues

Down on the pavement, watching those tail lights run away.
Down on the pavement, watching those tail lights run away.
Feeling my hurts and wondering who I know that could say.

(Chorus) Why? Why? Why is life like a hit-and-run driver?

Met him in Milwaukee, gone by the time we got to Rome.
Met him in Milwaukee, gone by the time we got to Rome.
Try it and buy it, but the price never gets you home.

Chorus

Sipping at a warm beer, listening to the chatter all around me.
Sipping at a warm beer, listening to the chatter all around me.
I know it doesn't matter—they're only talking philosophically.

Chorus

(Bridge) Sweet Sanity, the hours I spend with you!
Heart full of the grace of the Lord,
You always pull me through.
Pull me through.

Praying in the darkness, feels like the middle of the night.
Praying in the darkness, feels like the middle of the night.
Don't see things too clearly, Lord—praying hard for the light.

Chorus

I wrote this in September of 1980, after Jim McCarty, my Mick, drove off on his way to volunteer for Paul Shockley's group, Cosmic Awareness, in Oregon. We had become lovers that summer, after I cleared that with Don, with whom I had had a celibate relationship since 1971. When Mick left, I was flooded by many emotions! He returned for good on December 23, 1980 and joined L/L Research permanently then. He had felt the need to keep his word and help out the Windsong School there in Oregon, and is to be praised for that. However at the time it was hard catalyst to process! Writing these lines helped.

Sanity was Mick's truck at the time. He drove it to Oregon and back and had it until 1990, when he finally replaced it with his present vehicle, a Dodge Dakota named Sybil. We had some fine moments together in Sanity in the summer of 1980!

I Cry at Night

I cry at night,
Ask the Lord to hold me tight.
Oh, my Jim,
Something is gone in him.
My baby doesn't want me
Any more.

The silent type,
A steady, loyal guy,
He'd never leave.
He deeply cares for me.
But my cowboy doesn't want me
Any more.

I've got to ask how I just let
The sun go down?
What smog turned midnight's
Moonlight into foggy brown?
Or was it me at all?
I'm really rather swell.
Do I really have the power
To cause this fall?

He feels so old,
Though, to me, he shines gold.
He feels so sad.
The same things make me glad.
But my baby doesn't want me
Any more.

After Mick and I married in 1987 I went through a long, difficult spell of emotional weather. My physical body was in increasingly tough shape. In 1988 I had my gall bladder removed and in 1992, half my transverse colon, and these changes helped tremendously. Meanwhile my shoulders had crystallized and I could do almost nothing for myself. Mick faithfully cared for me, but for a good while he was emotionally distant and somewhat interested in another woman. It was a painful time, as these lines show. Fortunately, in 1996 it all turned around emotionally with us, and since then we have become closer and closer.

If I Had More Tears

If I had more tears I'd cry them for you.
If I had more heart I'd give it free.
I only have years of my time for you,
My only present is me.

(Chorus) Day by day—all the way—
You don't have to tell me you care
Days into weeks, and weeks into years
If you happen to look—I'll be there.

If I had the words to turn you around,
I'd spill them before you like flowers.
If joy or mirth touched your soul's cold bound,
I'd be laughing with you by the hour.
But my only words are for me.

Chorus

The sand never weeps in desert's dry land,
This spirit of yours is so very blue
But Spirit's my peace. And the shining band
Of angels that guards me guards you.
And my only tears are for me.

Chorus

I wrote this while Don was still alive, but unreachable by me, in 1984. His insanity took the form of psychotic paranoia and he was quite sure that I was not going to stay with him. In a way it seemed that was what he wanted, as he drove me from the room whenever he entered it, but keening and beating either the wall or his own body fiercely when he saw me. He only stopped the self-abuse when I left the room. It was excruciating for both of us, who still and always loved each other with all our hearts.

I'll Always Need You

(Chorus) I'll always need you.
I need you like I need the morning light.
Things may change; but we just reset our sights.
As long as you need me to, I will need you.

When we were new I needed you.
Your caring faith empowered me.
We worked as one in harmony.
You said the words, I set them down.
You were the motion, I the sound.
Together, we made history,
Witnessing to mystery.

Chorus

We'll always need to plant the seed.
We'll always wish for souls to fish.
We'll always need me. We'll always need you.
When I was down, you stuck around.
The doctors and the trips to town—
Remember, how I loved so strong
A sky-man who could not stay earthbound?

Chorus

Remember the before-time?
I was healthy, and full of rhyme.
You were silent and sly and dear.
You made you laugh, I held you near.
Then exercises, pills to take—
Most would toss me in the lake.
You were my hero, you did more—
You always kept me safe on shore.

Chorus

Illness made me zero, but you were my hero.
I couldn't sit, or lift, or stand,
Or write, or give a helping hand—
Dressing, bathing, washing hair,
If I needed—you were there—
You were gallant, you were kind
We kept us firmly on our mind.

Chorus

I wrote this on April 4, 1992. Don had died in 1984 and I found my health failing immediately thereafter. By the time Mick and I were married in 1987, I was very fragile and a year later I was bed-bound. My shoulders and neck were crystallized and I could not sit up straight or lift my arms above my shoulders. I was like a doll for Mick to dress and care for, and he did a wonderful job. Meanwhile, I did all I could to be of service, channeling, teaching and corresponding via tape letters. I did not discover computers or get back to vertical living until 1992. How I came to love the computer that made me useful as a writer again!

It is hard to say which words are about which man—Don and Mick—since they both cared for me as an invalid at times, and both were most loving, while often remaining unexpressive of the warmer emotions. These words are not at all descriptive of Mick now. When we began, however, there was no romance but only honor, respect and commitment to our spiritual work on the one hand and chemical attraction to sweeten the pot!

These were not easy times for us. But we saw it through, and love bloomed slowly, the wonderful, in-love kind, coming fully into our lives by 1994 or so.

I'll See You Again

I'll see you again.
Does it matter where or when?
Nature's time will flow
'Til time is one;
'Til time's kind will be done.

(Chorus) "Oh, so very special,"
I thought in my vague way.
I can't even say for sure
Just when you went away.

But now you're gone.
I carry on somehow
Hills and bills and TV on.
Goodbye for now.

I'll meet you one day,
Never say you've been away.
Orphans on the lawn—one day they're gone.
Swings empty where they played.

I'll see you again.
I'll be seeing you again.
I wait for you, pray for you.
I am your friend unto the end.

I wrote this on September 27, 1984. Don physically died on November 7, just a bit later. Tommy put it to music for Don's Memorial Service. His death was very difficult for me to bear. This was the first layer of feelings. There were many more. It took me about six years to begin to recover. I remember picking up a sheet of paper I did not recognize late in 1990 and finding that it was a first draft of the year's upcoming Christmas letter. Reading it through, I thought, "I like this person." That was the moment of true new life for me. And it has been like a whole different incarnation; as though I was born anew—two lives lived completely within one physical incarnation.

Loving You Hasn't Been Easy

Loving you hasn't been easy lately,
Fearing you haven't been loving me.
Shall we go walking in the evening?
Shall we stop waiting to see?

(Chorus) Cherishing all the good times;
Trusting in love through the bad times.
Hope makes the darkness shine,
Bringing our hearts into loving rhyme.

One day we said, "Now is the right time
That we shall prune all the season's vines."
Shall we go walking in the vineyard?
Shall His vision repair the wine?

Chorus

(Bridge) Do you suffer? So does she.
Are you weary? So is he.
Jesus' followers fell asleep.
Though his need was fathoms deep
He prayed alone.
We do not pray alone

Love is a mystery too great for telling;
No way for buying, no way of selling.
Shall we go walking to dip from the well?
Shall our hearts sing like a bell?

Chorus

I wrote this for Don on August 21, 1984, when he was still alive in the body, but lost in his intellect and emotions due to a wasting mental disease the doctors called "psychotic depression with hallucinations". One day, we met, Don and I, on our staircase, I going up and he going down. Confused and hurting, I said, "Don, I miss you so!" He replied, "I miss me too."

It was a very tough time for us both, and one Don did not survive. He was so wonderful. He is wonderful still, just not on this physical plane of existence. He helps me tremendously on the inner planes, especially when I am tuning to channel.

My Mick

He shines like the sun
From the lighthouse
Of his body.
He is Christ's son
And Christ's knight
In my world.

He cleans his machine,
Wiping the grass
From his mower.
His face gleams
Molten gold,
My beloved.

I write this for Mick (my nickname for my husband, Jim McCarty) on June 8, 2009. I imagine I saw him out the window, cleaning his mowers after a hard day of work at Jim's Lawn Service.

Our beginnings were not without challenge! In September, 1980, Jim sold his homestead, Hummingbird Mountain, on the Jones Branch of Mullins Creek, locally called Joner. All summer he had been helping Don and me move from our Douglass Boulevard apartment to a 6-acre gentleman's farm on Watterson Trail in Louisville. Don and I had invited him to join us there, but he felt he had made a previous promise to volunteer for the group that channeled This Awareness, Cosmic Awareness Communications, headed by Paul and Roshanna Shockley and Vicky T. They were headquartered in Olympia, Washington, but Paul lived in Yamhill, Oregon and there they had started a home-school, the Windsong School of Awareness. Jim stayed in Yamhill in an old brown trailer he called Tootsie Roll.

Two months later he realized that his true home was with Don and me at L/L Research and he rejoined us on December 23, 1980. Jim was the key. Three weeks later we started receiving the Ra contact sessions.

Needless to say, I did not stay mad! In fact, till this day we have lived "happily ever after."

A Poem for Charlie

I walked into the length of the dark house.
The first thought was the ceiling,
Oystered into soil long ago, so far above,
But I could see the pattern gleam,
Tiny bug-like swirls of good, imprinted paper,
Brightening white then, dusk now

When I say to you
Something,
I see you feel my words.
My thought brands your thoughts.
And if I will be lion-fierce gentle
As I am now, lamb-beast,
You will always have fresh scars

The staircase went square up
Many stories, ungraceful, to the ceiling,
Not lovingly, lyrically curved,
Just tall.

When Christ was killed
The talk of the New Kingdom died.
Jesus had preached this himself, but it didn't happen,
And within three fortnights of years it had died,
Dying more slowly on the lips
Of those who suffered for this belief.

A divider of wood went round the hallway wall,
Not like the two-colored paint on cement school walls,
Separated cheaply halfway up to brighten things,
But like a policemen walking his crushing job away
Into the gray evening: expensive, well-carved dado—
Hard to see its workmanship in this light.

That I haunt others
Is easily understood when I explain
How often I haunt myself, and that I
Never use the rite of exorcism.

It was too dust-dark staring to be a home,
Too clean to be rented, too proudly cared for.
The wallpaper hung in the air

With little gray wings
And there were no windows

Consider the half-weard of Sule Skerrie,
Bedding with a human but not human.
"Selkies swim in' the fame," the song goes.
In seven years he claimed his child and left Norway,
Leaving her only money:
Incomplete.

Consider Sarai and Abram
Who earned Isaac, who laughed
And he was born, proof of two duty-spent lives.
They never spoke joy or cared tight:
Incomplete.

Consider these of past and present
And that they are incomplete.

I thought one of the roomers here
Had given me this number—
I met him at a funeral and we talked vaguely together.
The old, dim doors were all silent and closed.
I hoped I had the right address

The lawn had worn thin under the tree
Years before. Probably no one could remember grass there.
Not antique grandeur, just good, wood-lasted worth,
Not pretty, but—

I started up the high, brown stairwell, black-gray shadowed.
It didn't creak. Dust was disturbed
By my hesitant ascent
To begin to try the doors

The hard, yellow earth
Will be soft enough,
Washed with my hair
And your sea.

*I wrote this for Charlie Fothergill in 1963. I dated Charlie for almost
three years, my last three years of undergraduate college at U of
Louisville. Charlie was a fine man who graduated in English*

Literature and at present is teaching high school students English at Kentucky Country Day, a private coed high school in Louisville. We split up when he wished to marry and I did not, in the spring of 1964.

Recipe for Disaster

I once had a man
Loved me so much he wore swimming trunks
Under his doctor suit
In case I wanted a dip,

When I wouldn't have him,
He stole my old watchbands
And killed himself.

I am shocked, standing at the sink,
Scrubbing at my scorched, yellow pan.

I wrote this in 1976, about a lovely young man—16 to my 23—who was devoted to me throughout his teenage-hood, since he was a friend of Betty Hoagland's (I call her Beth) at high school, and so he began coming to our "Louisville Group" meditations in the mid-sixties. I was his first love. And he suffered because he could not have me as wife. My heart truly went out to him.

What the reference to the pan is, I have no idea!

Sailor of Skies

He comes through the door
Breathing black-coat weariness.
His suitcases smell like Bangor,
Toledo, Montreal, Ft. Ord.
Dust, chill.
He puts them down
On the home ground,
Friendly turf and town,
Smells and smiles of home.
His own
Travel-stained papers
Flutter into their box,
Receipts of a life of labors
Grimed with loneliness, loss,
Lack of joy.

Welcome home, sailor of skies
You shall be perfect in my eyes

I wrote this in the early 1970s about Don Elkins, my beloved companion. He flew his routes with excellence and accuracy and took great pride in doing a top job. However he did it for a living and he got very tired of the concrete world of airports and motels. He was very glad to be home.

Shadow Song

To what can goodbye address itself?
Said after someone has departed,
Summing a circumstance now gone by,
It lingers, in the silence,
Like ashes after a fire
Or like brown stalks
Where flowers were.

Goodbye is not a reality.
Hello is not a reality.
They are only the small shadows
We cast upon each other.
And yet in smiles of greeting
And in tears of farewell,
How many parts may we add
To our stores of reality?

I will not turn yet
From the shadows.
I will cast my net
And seine my harvest of sorrow:
And sing this to the air.

*I wrote this on November 17, 1969, when the sting of Don Elkin's
retraction of his proposal of marriage was still quite fresh and painful.*

Six Poems for Don

(Originally titled "Six Poems from Me to You with Love")

I

Shy, quicksilver boy, silently hiding;
Sky man, part of heaven,
Meticulous, petulant, intractable,
Flashing with wisdom,

You open your eyes to me
And you see where I am,
And what matters to me matters also to you.

Long-boned, difficult, funny human,
Full of dignity, with the deep quiet of your eyes
You see me.

I see you too
And know you,
And cherish all that you are.

II

Godspeed in the year to come, my comrade.
I pledge my resources to your aid,
Both the creativity and the discipline.
I accept your ambitions as my ambitions.
What blessing I can invoke I hereby invoke
On the days to come, on all your dreams, and on you.

One thing: if we make it big,
And the money is rolling in,
How do we get the Creator his share?
I guess he'll have to take it out in trade.

III

Give me your burdens,
For well I know how to carry them.
And then give me your hand
And my step will be ever light.

What will I give you in return?
Will you only see for me

When my eyes are dim with tears?
Will you furnish me with
Your clear sight?

And in the exchange of our gifts
Will we not both see well the road we travel?
Will we not both walk it more lightly?

IV

My love is like a pale, pale vine
That grows along the ground
And hides his face within the shade
And turns his leaflets down.

My love has vocal cords of lead,
A voice like sounding brass,
And when his singing fills the air,
It breaks out panes of glass.

His ear is made of solid tin;
His taste in music's odd.
He dislikes all those cultured airs.
(We call him Ichabod.)

My love's so tall that when I put
My arms around his waist,
With six and one-half feet of him,
I lose sight of his face.

Although for cats and dogs and me
He's quite liable to fall,
With miscellaneous relatives
He'll have no truck at all.

My love can order me about
As though I were quite dumb,
And when I manage well, of praise
I may not get a crumb.

His fund of warmth reminds me of
A polar expedition.
It's so long since we kissed. I fear
He's quite out of condition.

Yet how I love my pale, pale vine
That creeps along the ground
And spends his days within the shade
And turns his leaflets down.

V

What this planet has in mind for us
Is that we should give up on each other.
We should say to each other, "There is no love here.
You scorn me by implication."

When we were children we may have expected
Prince Charming and Snow White.
Why you put up with me now
I don't know, but I know why I put up with you.

It is a matter of some importance to me
To be in the same ball park with you;
To be of service to you and to rest in your
Understanding.

And the implications of scorn between us
Are false, for we do not scorn each other.
We are only continuing to discover the equilibrium
Of warmth and coldness, expressions of our polarity.

Should I change? Should you?
Even if we could: no. Not at all.
This is our own thing.
This is our own time.
Not Prince Charming,
Not Snow White,
Not perfection,
But ourselves.
In the same ball park.

I am on your side.

VI

Each time that I say good-bye to you
I am well content.
If it were the last good-bye
I would remain well content.

The austere beauty of your steadfast soul
Remains always with me.

I would never have asked so much of any man
As you have freely given me:
In the sunlit reaches of my mind you have
Articulated fidelity; you have defined fidelity.
You have been wholly with me,
And that unspoken sacrament of presence
Remains and will remain with me.
I am well content.

And I wish only that if by my clumsy ways
I have caused your spirit pain,
I may pray that your pain may be healed
By my own constancy to you, which is absolute,

And by the endless turning of compassionate
Eternity.

*I wrote this for Don for Christmas in 1970. It was my gift to him that
year. Did he like it? I'll never know! But it gave me a chance to
articulate the complex feelings I had for him. I adored that man. He
was my Beloved Companion. And he still is that.*

Song for B.C.

In this whole wide world there are lots of girls and boys with whom I play,
And I carry on in the dusk and dawning and right on through the day.

(Chorus) But when I want to dream, I think of you. And when I want to scheme, I talk to you.
And when I'm lost, like a ship that's tossed, then you are home to me.

Sometimes memories seem to give me reasons to fear what's new and free,
All my attention in one dimension where there's no love for me.

Chorus

In your love I've had both the good and the bad, the sadness and the joy.
Though it's been uneven, I'll not be leaving your loving. You're my boy.

Chorus

B.C., short for Beloved Companion, was my nickname for Don. He liked it because no one ever guessed what the initials meant, yet he knew!

I wrote this in the seventies, and Tommy put it to music for one of our story-songs-gifts to Mom and Dad around 1980.

Suite to Unfinished Beginnings

(Original typescript noted here "For RWC.")

I

The Raw Materials

I came to the rattling mound of memories
For a search, my lost love,
Because I was alone
Last night and the Dipper
Poured the moon into a lost promise
Floating empty across my shattered white eyes.

You and I shaped times which had quiet actuality;
And now I have a quiet time too,
But I am alone,
Because I can look no longer
At the shining shapes
Of the crystal people at the party.
My white eyes flinch at the delicate, handblown hardness.

There is an exhibition Tuesday, an informative evening;
I shall go see it with a companion
Because I shall be alone
And would not choose to be alone
Without a companion whose eyes are livid and broken
And will not drown me in the shape of my caring.

There is a valley amid the chaos
Of foothills which has an orchard
We are all alone there –
And the fruit of each tree is a white fruit
Which is never plagued and never eaten.
The trees root in pain and stretch towards any sky.

II

Affirmation

Like a welcome wind on wet, sedge earth.
You disturb me with peace and growing; you stir
A restless life in the spring field,

Brown and beating as my hair would be
If it were new grass and I, earth.

Let us not speak of love. Love split us both once,
And poured us away. I receive your need,
Which is not desperation but a cry,
You calm cry, "I, you and I,"
And I answer, "Yes, always yes;

You are yourself whom I touch in reverence
With myself." At deep times, softly
Have you wrapped me strand by strand,
And held me, bundled quiet, in your hand.

III

The Unspeakable Theme

The most accursed word is love;
The most meaningless, the most useless.
The polemical , accusing, "Do not love me."
The begging, pitiful, "Do, do."
It is not possible to use the word nakedly.
All words are complicators,
Destroyers of the simplicity of touch.
Mouths are of the body. It is not meet
That they should become red-caverned maws
Spewing up the barriers minds build.
All words are immoral and indecent,
And the most despicable word is love.

The bright bruised sunset is dead. We saw it dead
And at the time felt only a small coldness
That death should exist. Our feelings
Were not sufficient. It was only later,
At the inappropriate time, that we grew frightened
And patched our fearful dreams into a funeral.
Death has never stained the morning
Or noon, nor will it ever, except in men's minds.

IV

Unpoetic Lyric

There is a time, golden father,
Strident son, when eyes
Become unlearned, laughter undidactic.
This time is the true time, far from poetry,
Poetry being the record of displacement, not fulfillment,
Time when the easy lemon and salt
Are follies chuckled from the mind
By the clean rapids of intense reality.

We have seen many things, blessed exulter,
Dear complainer, and all things we see
Are what we asked to see; all are good.
Others have chosen myths and precedents
To dress their dreams, but we remain newcomers
And use only what we make up,
And honesty, and affirmation, and each other.

The huddled boatman had rowed his uncaulked dory away
With straining back, aiming at tomorrow's ocean.
We had shipped the oars in our raw boat
And joined today rolling akimbo on the present pier:
We are not strangers.

Finding through other people's planetary traffics
You, star, I let me like a sun come down hard to warm
You. Oh genuine man, in the time of my flame
You have given me a place of haven.

V

Unfinished Beginnings

Beginnings are like peaches
In the icebox. They get soft
And noisome after a time.
You find them there, rotting,
And carry the aging mass to the tin garbage can,
Thinking, as you throw them away, that
Somewhere
You've seen a recipe that tells how,

If you ripened and processed this fruit
In a secret, right manner,
Which you've forgotten,
You could fill a cut glass decanter
With sparkling brandy.

It doesn't matter that the tin lid rattles loose.
You needn't close it tightly anyway.
Sometime,
Everyone comes back
And looks inside again
To see what he can salvage

I met Rick Crampton when I was a freshman at the University of Louisville. When Jim DeWitt and I agreed to work together to become "Jim and Carla" and sing folk songs which we created, that year, it was to Rick's studio, located on the second story of his mother's home, we went for rehearsals. Jim DeWitt was proficient with the guitar and liked to use a Gibson twelve string with "silk and steel" strings. His double-bass voice was unusual in that it had no harshness, and he sounded like a baritone even when he went very low. Jim's and my voices blended with an uncanny beauty, and we became very good folk singers indeed in the course of three years' practice, spending every Saturday morning in Rick's studio. He often recorded us, and I still have CDs of our work together which Rick sent me in later years, when he retired.

When I was 13, and again when I was 15, I was bedbound for months with failed kidneys. During those times I kept myself busy collecting songs from the Childe ballads, the Sharpe ballads and the Lomax songbooks, among many others. I also collected poems that took my fancy, mostly Irish poetry of the nineteenth century, which Jim and I put to our own music. I kept notebooks of these lyrics, some of which I still have, and we made up many original tunes for the old words when no music was given for them. We also covered songs written by popular folk singers of the time like Bob Dylan.

After Jim chose not to accept our offer to tour as the opening act for Peter, Paul and Mary in 1964, I stopped working as a folksinger. But when Jim's and my marriage came unglued in 1968, I began to date Rick off and on during that summer, and then, years later, he was my lover occasionally during the nine years in which Don asked for a celibate relationship with me. Don and I had talked this through, and he was OK with this arrangement. We were very discreet. Though Rick's visits with me were few and far between, his genuine affection, expressed physically, sustained me mightily as a woman, and I am forever thankful for him.

As the years passed Rick wooed his Dianne and married. However he and I retain to this day a solid long-distance friendship that now includes Dianne, whom I have come to love a lot.

I wrote these poems in the early fall of 1964, after Rick and I tried being engaged for all of five days and found that we would never fit together well at that level of mutual commitment. Rick's gifts to me were an appreciation of me that was totally authentic, and an inner sensitivity that rendered him a keenly perceptive lover of beauty. He and I shared the beauty of music, places, works of art and literature and each other.

Rick worked for many years for Glen Glenn Studios, doing sound work for television, and collecting awards aplenty for his work during his long career. He now dwells in Maine in the house he and Dianne worked on themselves, and on which he was sort of "general contractor", with his beloved wife, Dianne.

Three Minor Thoughts for Don

If we knew what next we'd do
Then age would hold us tight.
If we could spy the reason why,
We would have wisdom's sight.
Now, as to who, that's me and you,
And I love us, through and through.

I propose we help others;
You give out the spaceships.
I'll make the songs.

If my elbows were wings I would fly to you
And thank you.
When I was alone without you,
I did not know how to be alone.
Present solitude finds me steady.
You taught me that. Here is my Valentine!

I wrote this on June 2, 1970. I was delighted with Don at my side, and determined to find a steady way to enjoy being with him on his terms—unmarried and simply together. I always wistfully wished for marriage, being very conventional in that way. However, for Don I explored less conventional forms of companionship, I think to very good effect.

To Don in the Hospital

Your praise is the song of my soul;
Your beauty, my burden of joy.
If you will, stay a while,
For the carriage comes rolling too soon.
We must leave by the light of the moon.
Make me smile

We are the fortunate two
For we've always been our girl and boy
By our sides let us stay
For the carriage comes rolling too soon.
We have only this farewell tune.
Hold me close.

(Bridge) We shall run a good race as we leave from this place
We have found joy from strife and made a good life
Truth from life; love from strife.

The course of our race is begun,
My praises will always be yours.
If you will, stay a while,
For the carriage will roll all too soon
And we'll count every cost as a boon.
Let me stay with you and
Make you smile.

This poem was written on July 6, 1984, during the time Don was in Norton Hospital for five weeks. He was suffering greatly, mentally and emotionally, and so was I. It was a hard lesson for me to learn, that my love could not rescue him from his inner nightmare. This time apart literally broke our hearts.

Why Did You Do Me This Way Blues

Now you just packed your bags,
Your raggy, taggy bags.
You left me your old bills
And my brand-new ills.
Why did you do me this way?

Darlin', tell me why
Did you do me this way?
You forgot your teef
Cause they're a-stickin' out my beef!
Why did you do me this way?

(Chorus) Why did you do me this way?
Why did you do me this way?
Why'd you get up and go?
Darlin', tell me just why?
Why'd you go and do me this way?

You left without a word,
Not even one little word.
Guess you knew I'd say
What would make you stay.
But why'd you do me this way?

Chorus

Now, honey, you were rude.
You really were so rude!
Don't let me be misconstrued:
You were downright crude.
Why did you do me this way?

Chorus

I'm getting out my shoes,
My hulking hiking shoes.
You know I paid my dues.
I'm shaking of these blues,
But—Honey—now come on—
Tell me—
Why did you do me this way?

I wrote this the spring after Don died, on March 11, 1985, feeling so lost without him.

Why Do I Love You?

(Chorus) Why do I love You like I do?
Why do I love You like I do?
Why do I love You—and oh! how I love You—
Why do I love You like I do?

Chorus

Please, Lord, I want to understand
How You can be lost from the heart of a man?
When every leafy bower,
Every bee and flower is praising You,
Just as I do too.

Chorus

(Bridge) It's a wonder just to take Your hand;
Just to feel Your dear Self by me.
The nearest, dearest thing I ever felt
Has been my love for You.
I need my love for You.

There you are, in a smiling face,
And there you are in our hungering race,
How do we keep living
Without the love You're giving,
Without the chance to love you too?

Chorus

Don't need to tell me; I know the pain.
I know the songs of sorrow, the stress and the strain
But when I've lost my way,
You will touch my soul and say,
"Peace be with you."

Chorus

When you are silent, it's plenty that You're there
When I am listening, it's glory that You share
Oh! How can we keep breathing
When we're not receiving
The love that you offer ever new?

Chorus

I do not know when I wrote this. All my life, as long as I can recall anything, I recall the yearning for my Beloved that seems to me to define my nature.

You Are Home to Me

(Song for B.C from me.)

In this whole wide world, there are a lot of girls
And boys with whom I play,
And I carry on in the dusk and dawning,
And right on through the day.

(Chorus) But when I want to dream, I think of you,
And when I want to scheme, I talk to you,
And when I'm lost, like a ship that's tossed,
Then you are home to me.

Chorus

Sometimes memories seem to give me reasons
To fear what's new and free—
All my attention in one dimension
Where there's no love for me.

Chorus

In your love I've had both the good and the bad,
The sadness and the joy.
Though it's been uneven I'll not be leaving
Your loving. I'm your boy. (Originally, "You're my boy")

Chorus

This was a poem written for Don on August 2, 1978. Don seldom spoke, either to compliment or judge me. Yet I felt entirely at home from the very first, safe, sound and cherished, in his silence. He ducked my compliments, and when I looked for an endearment for him, I told him I would call him B.C., and only he would know that it meant "Beloved Companion". He liked that, and wiggled his left ear at me in thanks. I adored that man!

Metaphysical Poetry

All of the Circular Time

Down comes the rain
And out comes the sun,
And another cycle of life is begun.
Down comes the dark
And up pops the light,
And a thousand beauties to bless before night.
You can't say, "Thank you", enough times
Especially when going through rough times.
Thank you, praise you, bless you Lord.
Thank you for the cycles.
Thank you for change.
Thank you for losses.
Thank you for gains.,
It's all the same.
It's all so fine,
We thank you, Lord
All the time—
All of the circular time!

*I wrote this on November 1, 1988, a happy ditty for the very happy
year after I married Jim McCarty. Illness was with me, and soon
would have me completely bed-bound, but even then I was a fairly
happy camper. I very much enjoyed—and still do—being married.
I'm conventional enough that the status means a lot to me
emotionally.*

Beautiful Day

It's a beautiful day,
The sun is beaming,
Salt marsh full of silver minnows—
It's a wonderful day,
Sunshine
Why do I feel as if I'm being winnowed
On such a beautiful day?

I can read my books—
I've got a hundred.
I could go for a long, brisk walk.
It's a wonderful day,
Friends and kindred,
Why do I feel like there's no one to talk to
On such a beautiful day?

If I could look, look around me
And forget about me, forget about me,
If I could fix my gaze to see
You everywhere, in the sun, sand and sea
You everywhere, everywhere.

This poem was written at Pawley's Island, South Carolina, where there was a salt marsh not far from our rented vacation home. Any time Mick and I crossed the bridge from island to mainland there would be fishermen there, trying their luck. The date was probably 1985, shortly after Don died.

Black and Blue

A band of black geese is flying
Against the sky
The light is gray and dying.
I watch with empty eyes.
Where do they all go?
Do they seek summer?
When the cold wind blows
Do they still hope it's warm somewhere?
Standing on this path,
I keep my hands warm by blowing.
Wind comes from the west.
My heart is crying, too cold for going.

(Chorus) Once we were clean and new.
What did we ever do
To get so black and blue?

My lady touches me, smiling,
Without a word,
Her fingers bright and beguiling.
Her breath is softly heard.
Then the years pass away.
She smiles no more.
Though my lady she stays,
She cannot find the man she loved before,
In my heart I reach out,
Beg for her romancing.
I will never forget
My lady loving, glancing, dancing.

Chorus

The fog rolls in from the river
And fills my mind.
Is God an Indian giver?
Am I the one that's blind?
I throw my dice to the wind,
Truth, beauty and caring.
Like straws, they fall from my hands
Do I still hope my love's worth sharing?
Staring, lost in a maze,

Friendly voices are shouting.
I am in such a daze
That I can't hear them, deafened by doubting.

Chorus

I wrote this for a story with songs I was doing with my brother, Tommy. I believe it was either This is the Day *or* The Journey. *I was thinking about my Mom and Dad when I wrote it. They loved each other a lot, but until later in life it was seldom at the same time. When Mom grew older she permanently scorned Dad sexually. He accepted her decision and they found, in their later years together, a very amicable friendship.*

The Bright Bruised Sunset

The Bright bruised sunset is dead.
We saw it dead
And at the time felt only a small coldness
That death should exist. Our feelings
Were not sufficient. It was only later,
At the inappropriate time,
That we patched our dreams into a funeral.
Death has never stained the morning
Or noon, nor will it ever,
Except in men's minds.

I know I wrote this during my college years, which were 1961 through 1965. It is likely that it is a poem of grieving after Don MacKenzie jilted me at the altar in September 1962. I was sad and grieving for three years or so after he left me. As Cat Stevens said it so well, "The first cut is the deepest."

Caving

I just got to go to caving,
Hoping love can find me there.
Got to go down in the caverns,
Scuffling sightless through the rubble,
Catch and kill the white blind fishes,
Find the darkness black and bare,
Drink my bones in limestone taverns.
All those colors, that's my trouble,
Smother me in rainbow wishes.
Going back where it's black.
Sightless eyes make me wise.

(Chorus) Close your eyes, my darling.
Let it all go by.
Drop your brush and palette.
Let your spirits fly.
Down to the sun
Where we lose so much.
Where we learn to touch

(Coda) We're one.
We're one.
We're all one.

I wrote this for the song-story The Journey, *which I wrote and Tommy and I sang together on a particularly bad recording as a Christmas present for our parents around 1979. We re-did the song on the album, of the same name, later in Washington D.C. at Dusk and Dawn Productions. It is about prayer, which feels to me like entering a cave of sorts within myself. I went to Mammoth Cave when I was a six-year-old, and at that time the park staff would row us into the underground stream and shine their flashlights so we could see the albino fishes that lived there. Over the centuries these fish had lost their ability to see, as there was no light. The fish is a symbol for Christianity.*

Children of Eternity, Children of the Lord

There are many things in life I wish I'd done a different way.
I feel regret for every smile I didn't smile, every kindness I've
forgot.
It doesn't weigh me down. I know it's just humanity.
We are sinners, all. Life's not an illness, but the visual aid
For conditioning the children of eternity who wait within.

I rejoice in being able to try to offer shelter
To the souls that are mine to keep—
Souls gone on, whose wholeness only now I see;
Souls now present and so closed to me
In undecipherable ways.

But I make mistakes, from the first and last,
Predictable and wrong. I quit often.
But as I sit and sing my hymns,
I feel that Presence within. My heart is a tabernacle,
And I am a child of eternity.

Stranger in a strange place
Made of bits of time and space
When our time and space are o'er
We'll be children of eternity;
Children of the Lord.

*I do not recall when I wrote this but guess it to be around 1987, the
year I married Jim McCarty. When we married we had the issue
between us of his distance in an emotional sense and his desire to
remain distant. The love was there, but the trust came much more
slowly.*

Children of My Thoughts

Children of my thoughts,
I speak to you with some embarrassment,
For there are those among you I would
Rather not have looking so healthy.

You, child of my lust, you're looking very well.
I give you more than adequate nourishment, don't I?

And you, child of my reaching hands,
You'll have me in a bind one day.

Have you noticed, children of my desires,
That the family is much too large?
Its food is costing us dearly!

I cannot recall when I wrote this, but from its form I would guess it was in the mid-1970s.

Cottage in the Mountains, Cottage by the Sea

I have a little cottage in the mountains.
I have a little cottage by the sea.
The sea is lover to me in the summertime.
The mountains in the cold times hold my dreams.

(Chorus) I skip over water,
I dance over sea,
And all the birds in the air
Can't catch me.

Getting to my cottage isn't easy.
Living life awake can make you cry.
The sea is lover to me in the summertime,
Caressing into stillness my loud, "Why?"

Chorus

Beloved, O Beloved, when it's winter
At my mountain cottage you shall be.
Pine and oak cathedral, and the large view,
And the dream that is turning into me.

(Coda) "I will lift up mine eyes unto the hills,
Whence cometh my help."[1]

I wrote this on August 24, 1985, while Mick and I were vacationing at Pawley's Island, South Carolina. I was always healed and restored by proximity to the ocean there, and I remember composing this poem there by South Carolina's lovely waters. The Chorus is taken from an old folk song.

---

[1] This text is part of Psalm 121.

A Delft White Girl

A delft white girl went down a path
With sunlight tangling through her long brown hair,
And dust was in the air above the dusty path.
The bright sun showed how long the path went bare;
And over a spring-treed hill the long-backed sheep had mowed,
A whispering rooster crowed.

The delft white girl with dark elf locks
Turned from the sun to sit on a flat black stone
That lay in wet-leaved shade on stream-bank rocks,
Took out a black brush made of fur and bone,
Hair in broken feathers down her curled white knees,
And gathered her hair to sheaves.

The pebbles slipped, the rooster wept,
A brown, burned boy came slipping down the bed.
Without ado, he said, "Pull back that hair unkempt.
Don't bend and brush hair over your eyes," he said,
"I'll give you a starched white cap to roach your hair,
Else you'll not see what's there."

He pointed up the road and said,
"Do not think you are part of Irvington,
Or Brandenburg, or Muldraugh Hill, or home, or bed—
Think always only that you must be gone
To where you never were. Think not of places,
But of cocks calling races."

He sidled up the shadowed stream,
Beckoned with a short, bright leaf he'd found,
And slid away like a dusty bird from a slight, tan dream.
She stood up into the white light, heard the sound,
And thought she'd not been here, would not be there, this morning,
But was always now becoming.

I wrote this poem in 1963 after a road trip with Charlie Fothergill to a restaurant in Corydon, Indiana, downriver on the Ohio by an hour's drive. The place-names are from around that area in Kentucky, across from Corydon.

At the time I was actively engaged in singing folk songs with Jim DeWitt, whom I married in November, 1964. You can see the sensibility of the old Childe Ballads in the feel of this poem. DeWitt and I never put this to music, however.

In editing this I only added punctuation.

The Distance Between

African Woman, African man, people starving on the desert sand.
Indian maiden, Indian child, American Natives hungry, drunk
and wild.
Well I know it's wrong, and my feeling's strong,
But I know about the distance between.

(Chorus) The distance between—you know it's just illusion.
But the reason change
Is hard to arrange is,
It hurts so in the distance between,

Nelson Mandela, Bishop Tutu, holding off old from destroying
the new,
Holding off new from destroying the old, trying to give love that
the world can't hold.
Well, I know apartheid could never be right,
But I know about the distance between.

Chorus

Look at the faces on our city streets, people we may know, and
they've nothing to eat,
People on welfare, they want to blow, but they can't afford to,
pay's too low.
Well it makes me sad, and it makes me mad,
But I know about the distance between.

Chorus

Let's build healing! Let's take on change! Hey, you big bully, I've
got your range.
People in shipwreck, plan crash, car wreck; people maimed past
the skill of doctor-tech.
Well, we run the straight race, keep a smile on our face,
But we know about the distance between.

*I remember writing this on February 9, 1991. It was part of my
United Thank Offering letter to Calvary's parishioners that year. I
was the UTO officer for Calvary for quite a few years, starting in the
preceding year.*

Dreamers

Have you known a dreamer? His eyes are strangely keen.
His vision sights a different world than we have ever seen.
His gaze strikes fear in people's hearts. They think he reads their
minds.
And so he does, and plays his part, and acts so very kind.

(Chorus) We must cherish the dreamers,
Nurture them, care for them
For without them our rainbows never have an end.
And dreamers dream of the minted gold
That lies at the end of the magic arc drawn in the sky.
We must cherish the dreamers.

Jesus was a dreamer. He dreamed the perfect dream.
He came to Earth of human birth to share His love supreme.
He gave His all to dream for us, to die and then to rise,
To make a real world for us who share the dreamer's eyes.

Chorus

*I wrote this about Don, and it shows a lot of my understanding of him
and his place in my heart. I did not idolize Don, but I knew his
greatness, depth and wisdom, his compassion and understanding. Who
could not admire such a wonderful man among men?*

The End of the World

She doesn't say a word, just leaves the room,
Stands at the kitchen window, plaiting her heavy hair.
I say, "Don't be absurd, you're not marooned.
Everyone knows and loves you."
She's nodding in bleak despair.

(Chorus) Looking out the window,
Gazing at the sails all furled,
Swaying slow in sorrow,
Looking for the freedom
At the end of the world.

Voyagers' songs see far. The high notes ring,
Keening the hope, "Tomorrow," gentling the past time closed.
She lilts the age-old airs. Her true voice sings
Of love always given, not borrowed;
Of giving she freely chose.

Chorus

Her memory haunts the waters, sailor become,
Faring in strangers' kingdoms, rowing in effortless whorls.
She is nobody's daughter, nobody's son.
Easy to love in freedom the ocean at the end of the world.

Chorus

*I wrote this on September 30, 1983, after I came home from vacation
in late at Pawley's Island in late August. Don's behavior had begun to
be a little "off" for him, and I was off-balance that fall, sensing
trouble to come. Part of me just wanted vacation's peace again. But
that was not to be. In the next year we moved to a farm near Atlanta,
then back to Louisville five months later, and we continued to
endeavor to do Ra sessions. A bit more than a year later, Don was
gone, lost to suicide. There were no more Ra sessions. But it was not
vacation at all. I was in mourning ahead of time, somewhere in the
recesses of my unconscious mind, the mind that knows when there is
nothing to know.*

Feet of Clay

(Chorus) Floating so gently through realms of infinite day,
Heart of an angel caught into this world with feet of clay.

Life is like a dime store. First you choose
And then you pay the price, wrap it up and take it home.
And if it's broken you can try to take it back
But, "Listen, Mac," the lady says, "No guarantees."
Feet of clay.

Chorus

We are beautiful inside. We love and care to do
The right things, laugh, and pray and sing.
Then we go out into the world
And all the people come our way, they all have feet of clay
Feet of clay.

Chorus

What is the nature of a man?
We never live up to the plan that we can understand.
Knowing what is good, we do the bad
And yet I know we're good, we just have feet of clay.
Feet of clay.

Chorus

I wrote this poem in July 1978, while creating the story-with-songs,
The Journey. *My brother Tommy and I recorded this on the album
of the same name. The tune is his.*

Gifts

Life is a mystery.
This is truest certainty.
But we can give the history
Of our hearts in love.
Love has had so many names,
So many faces, so many claims
That don't fit hand in glove.

(Bridge) Not to our eyes will the mirror speak.
Only do we have what we perceive.
And so we give the gift of ourselves
Because that is all we have to give.

(Chorus) We each hear a different name,
And love, to me is Jesus
Because I hear this voice;
Because I took his hand;
Because, to me, He came.

We are a mystery
Wrapped within a quiddity.
Still, we brothers, sisters be,
One in heartfelt love.
Jesus becomes my life.
Jesus becomes my Self.
My Self, I give in love.

Chorus

I live the life I'm given.
I share the love I'm bidden.
But all reality is hidden
Behind all that we can see,
Yet that is all there is.
In this mystery, I'm the gift,
The one receiving, the one bereft—
All these things are me.

Chorus

This is not wisdom.
This is just all there is.
In cruelty, in frailty,

We kill, we save, we take and give.
All that I give is to my Self,
Whom I've not known
And do not know
And never expect to know completely.

(Bridge) We are the fire.
We are the smoke.
We are the ashes.
We are the nothing
In the mystery of love.

Call this love by any name,
Take within the self to reign
In doubt and fear and doubt again.
The All that is All is the same.
Leave behind the false and true.
Mystery will leave no clue.
But all you are will only come true
When you heed love's name.

I cannot recall writing this, but it is dated September 2, 1991, when I was in the very worst of my difficulties with my GI tract. Half of my transverse colon was removed in early 1992. I was in a world of hurt until then, which never has kept me from having spiritually uplifting moments such as this poem's writing indicates, and for that I am very grateful indeed. For me, the intensity of severe physical pain has sometimes rendered me unusually open to such moments of transcendent joy.

I Sat Beneath a Tree

I sat beneath a tree to ease my mind;
To smell the sweet smell of the leaves so dark and kind;
Thinkin' 'bout the years gone by; wonderin' if I'll find
It's hard to leave the laughter of my childhood far behind.

I thought about the times we had in spring—
The songs, the fire rose swiftly higher than birds upon the wing.
We shared almost everything that every moment brings
Touching hearts and hands, so full of love for what is gone

(Chorus) So full, so full, so full of love.

I sat beneath a tree and tried to pray.
A tear from memories sad and sweet was bein' brushed away.
But then the Father came to me and gave me eyes to see
That in each sad and happy day, He is here always.

In fantasy, I saw all time as one,
My future friends and wisdom mingling with what's passed and
done,
And always He who takes my soul and, touching, makes it whole,
Full of love for what is to come

Chorus

*When Tommy was a senior in high school he went on a camping trip
with his very best friends and had a memorable time. He told me
about it and I wrote this song for him in 1978. Tommy was born in
1957 and graduated high school in 1974. He put lovely music to my
words and it is recorded on a songs-and-story creation we did together
called* This Is the Day.

I'm A Cup

I'm a cup, Lord. Fill me up, Lord.
I want You to live my day.
I want Love to have its say.
Fill me up to the top! Fill me up.

I came out of sleep with this ditty in my head and wrote it down in 2008. After I jotted it down, I forgot all about it! It is a feel-good fragment, very fine for tuning.

It Is from the Resting

It is from the resting that the reason comes.
While the March wind is blowing with no sound
Things fly from touch. Grapples drop away
When we dream.

It is from the losing that the gain is won.
While the games are playing Refiner's Fire
Body drops away, grapples fly overboard.
Sea of Dreams.

It is from these limits that the ocean sets
That many rules are changing. Rest in listening.
Hollow body now. Ready for the flow.
Ocean, Love.

The original typescript has a subtitle as follows: "On The Occasion Of The 3-Week Cold *clrm 3-10-97". When you stack the symptoms of a bad cold on top of the aches of a rheumatoid arthritic and the GI-tract spasms of a woman suffering undiagnosed and untreated gall bladder and transverse colon woes, you can begin to figure that I was feeling pretty rocky! As I grow older and as more of my friends find themselves in discomfort from various diagnoses, I appreciate these thoughts more and am glad to share them.*

It Is Good

It is good to mark the passage of time,
To end and begin again,
To honor the days as if they were wine,
To savor and praise your friends.

There is health in the seasons and sense in the days.
There is strength in connecting to earth.
For with all of our guile and our clever ways,
We shall end, and again come to birth.

I do not recall writing this little poem. It feels as though I wrote it in the seventies, and the typescript is from a typewriter, not a computer, so it's that old for sure.

I've Been Up All Night

I've been up all night waiting for you.
My eyes squeeze tight, listening for you.
Oh, how you speak! Thank you.

Living in the shotgun seat, out of control,
From the endless deeps
I surrender to joy. Thank you.

Did you think you were driving?
Surrender! Be made whole!
Thank you.

I am waiting for your Word!
How I love your Word!
Thank you.

I do not recall writing these verses, but the energy seems to be mine of the seventies, very mystical.

The Journey

The journey calls me, and I must go,
Though where it will lead me, I don't know.
Maybe I'll never know.
What am I doing? Is it wrong or right?
When shadows cross me, do I still fight?
I turn and they've faded from my sight.

(Chorus) The road is winding and long,
And everlasting is my love song.

Who am I seeking? Please show me Your face.
It comes in my visions and leaves no trace.
Maybe there'll be no trace.
And if my steps should lead me through some rocky times,
And I never really find You, I don't mind.
The Son of Love, Your Name You never sign.

Chorus

(Bridge) Jesus, it's lovely to love You.
It's being in love with love,
Being in love with love.
And all the faces that I see, of friends and strangers and you and me,
Are places where Your love dwells.
It tells me where to go.
It lets me know that all things will be well.
All things will be well.
Jesus Emmanuel!

The journey calls me and I must go,
But where it leads me, I don't know.
Maybe I'll never know.
But if my steps should lead me into rocky times
And I never really find you, well, I don't mind.
'Cause, Son of Love, Your name you never sign.

Chorus

I wrote the words to this eponymous song for our story-and-song tape,
The Journey, *given to Tommy's and my parents for Christmas*

around 1980. Tommy created the music. It remains one of my favorite of Tommy's and my collaborations.

Just a Small Tin Angel

My mother is an angel. My father is a star.
Like stepping stones I've walked the waves
I have come so very far, so very far

(Chorus) Just a small tin angel
With tinsel hair,
Crying so softly, "Stranger, don't despair.
Angels always care.

I am the wine behind your mind
That let you laugh in the breeze,
The sweet sand footprints by the sea,
The angel on your tree, your Christmas tree

Chorus

Angel live in gladness to touch a troubled mind,
To say, "Have hope, not sadness.
You'll leave this ragtime world behind,
So far behind."

Chorus

Beloved planet, swirled in mist,
Won't you ever understand?
I wrap you in my golden skirt
And offer you my hand,
I offer my hand

Chorus

I wrote the words to this and Tommy put the music to it around 1976. It was one of the songs on our song-and-story tape for our parents' Christmas.

The Lamb and the Zebra

The moon revolves around the sun.
The lightening shoots its shrouded gun.
The lamb and zebra go their way.
I lost my life for love today.
I told her life was just a play.
The play, my life, was done today.

Death is truly no different than life.
Its peace is just the same as strife.
The lambs and zebras here are souls.
They always were parts of the whole.
My love has killed herself and me,
Death is the same as life. She'll see.

We all revolve around the Lord.
He is the one enlightening Word.
There is no death or life to Him.
There is no sort nor kind nor kin.
The lamb, zebra, you and me,
The moon, the sun are one, you see

I remember writing this in my first home with Jim DeWitt when we married, a one-room apartment on Avery Court, very near U of L, with more roaches than windows. This entire court has now been demolished and the Music School built in its place. DeWitt and I lived there from November 1964, when we married, until the spring of 1965, when we took care of my parent's home while they were gone to Europe for Pop's engineering work. That lasted for 15 months. It was a difficult time for me. I was trying to grasp what had happened to all my good plans, with no luck!

Lament for Prisoners

You can't see the wall from the prison
And you can't see the prison from the wall.
I only go there on Fridays
But they can never get out at all.

(Chorus 1) Set me free, Lord, set me free!
Show me sky, Lord, tell my why.
Let me be,
Bye and bye.

He doesn't know the crime he committed;
Can't tell you when his sentence began.
I only go there on Fridays
But seven days a week, he's their man

Chorus 1

Some of his friends are on the outside.
They don't think much about him anymore.
I only go there on Fridays
And last time it was hard to find the door.

(Chorus 2) Drift away, Lord, drift away.
White on white, Lord, let me fly
Let me say
Bye, bye, bye.

I came that first Friday on an impulse.
I thought that I could help him pass the day.
I only come here on Fridays—
Time passes without me anyway.

Chorus 2

The turnkey has been so nice to me
He doesn't get many volunteers
I only come here on Fridays,
But I know how a prisoner disappears

Chorus 2

(Coda) But I only,
Only go on Fridays.

I remember writing this, and having strong feelings behind the writing. I am guessing I wrote this while my beloved Mother was caught in alcohol addiction in her middle age. That would put the date of writing in the mid-eighties.

Let Me

Let me
Remain, O Lord,
Not in a body or in a thought,
But in the air, as fragrance from
A flower.

Make me
A smile that fills
One lover's night with fire,
And forges one enduring bond
With light,

Or let
Me be a prayer
Come true: a famine quenched,
A husband home, a whole world grown
From war.

But, Lord,
If I deserve
To stop, and drown in earth
Because of times I which, on earth,
I sinned

Still, let
Me be, before
I die, to whom you will,
A crystalline absolute, a flame,
A gift.

I believe I wrote this shortly after the breakup of my first marriage in 1968. I came home in March from Canada and Don joined me that November. I wrote this sometime that summer, I think.

Like a Sailor on the Land

Like a sailor on the land
With the water beckoning so close to hand,
Yet the sailor home he stays,
"Cause his ship was sunk and he must earn his pay.
That's how my mind so often feels
As I grind my mental wheels,
But then suddenly my mind is freed
And it's roaming far at sea.

(Chorus) And then I praise the mystery
And welcome the epiphany.
That tells me my life will be.
Set free.

When I was a little kid
And my mommy called, will I just ran and hid.
Now I'm over twenty one
Duty calls me, hello gray skies, goodbye sun.
Now, I know it's just a platitude
But when I can stop my mind
Then my life is just an attitude.
That's the truth of what I find.

Chorus

All of us are looking for
All the freedom that we think life has in store,
Making money if we're poor
Getting smarter if we never knew the score.
But the freedom is inside our heads
When we let our souls be fed,
And there's laugher in the rafters
When our thoughts to love are lead

Chorus

I wrote this for the song-and-story piece, The Journey. *Tommy sang this on the finished "album" when we re-recorded the songs for publication in a CD of the same name. The date of writing was around 1980.*

Listening to Alejandro Escovedo

Come to the center.
Come in from the world.
Stand at last in the sun;
In the One.

Come to the center.
Come away from the masks.
Enter the doorway of your head
And the One

Come to the center.
Come away from the dream.
Focus into the reality of going
Into the One

Light of Light
Lord of all my days
Beloved
In you I am One
In you we are all One,
One,
One.

I have no recall of writing this poem and had to look up the courageous singer to whom the title refers. When I did, I brought back the memory of being in the car with Mick, going cross-country on the way to see Mom McCarty on October 28, 2006. Such good times the two of us have had, traveling. There is a little bubble of sheer bliss that surrounds us when we are away from anything known, between here and there, and enjoying each other.

My Friends

I have this friend, name of Jane, so beautiful in face.
She talks like Shakespeare changed his name, in words of wit and
grace.
My friend thinks she's around the bend with no ability at all.
In comforting brilliance, I have learned.
So much humility. What a gift, humility!

(Chorus) My friend, my friend,
He/She shows me the Creator.
God's love's never has an end,
It's flowing through the hands of my friend.

My friend, Joe, is suicidal;
Going to end it all.
His suite was marked 'First Class Bridal'.
But then he took a fall.
My friend, shivering, comes to me,
Frozen from the cold,
And I learn, while reaching out to him
The torture of his soul;
The love within my soul.

Chorus

My friend Linnie's got round heels—not in bed I mean.
The whole world uses her for wheels. She's rushing 'round the
scene.
She's doing about a thousand chores; still thinks,
"I'm not good enough."
In holding my friend close to me, I see the heart of love
I hold the selfless heart of love.

Chorus

Now, take my old friend, Herbie. He ran a pretty fast mile.
And though he never won the Derby, the roses were his smile.
Some folks are just so perfect, they float right on above.
And in his death, my friend still teaches me
To live my life so freely; to smile and act so fearlessly.

Chorus

In closing, I should mention a special friend, my Dad.
There might be times that he knocked the Ascension
But he's around when things get bad.
He's like the rock that cannot slip, solid in his sharing,
Gray hairs coming and a mean old hip,
He's constant in his caring.
I love him for his caring.

Chorus

(Coda) Sometimes I think that my friends are all gone
And darkness never will turn into dawn.
Then I notice my eyes are closed. My hands are folded, my heart morose.
So I open my eyes to see the sunrise
Lift up my heart to be a friend
To my friends

The people in the song are Tommy's and my friends, and our Dad. Jane was a close friend of mine for twenty years. We sang together in the Louisville Bach Society and I babysat her four kids. Linnie, another friend of mine since 1970 or so, shared with me a love of Don's aunt and uncle. Linnie lived with Marion and Martha, whom the family called, "Tot", for a time. Herbie and Joe were Tommy' friends. And we shared our Dad. This song was part of the writing for Tommy's and my mutual composition, The Journey. *He wrote the lyrics and I, the words, and we sang the songs and read the story together.*

The verses and Chorus were written on January 14, 1979, and the Coda was written two months later, on March 9 of the same year.

O Light of My Vision

O light of my vision,
You've seen me through the day.
Now night is upon me.
Keep me Yours, I pray.

(Chorus) I'm so lost until I remember you!

It's a very peculiar world.
It changes every hour.
Now it's fresh, now it's spoiled,
Doomed to frost, the flower.

Chorus

(Bridge) Almighty God, heavenly Father, We give Thee
Humble and hearty thanks and praise.
Throughout our pilgrimage of days.

O flame for my tempering,
You honed me in the fire.
Action's now behind me.
Was I true in my desire?

Chorus

I so want to love and give
My heart to those with me,
But did I humbly, gently, live
The day you prepared for me?

Chorus

I wrote this on September 17, 1992, and rewrote it on November 5th, not quite two months later. I do not recall writing it. So often, these poems simply flow through me when I am tuned to a certain frequency of meditation, prayer or contemplation, and then it's just a rush to grab pen and paper and get the words down.

The Ocean at the End of the World

She doesn't say a word,
Just leaves the room.
Stands at the kitchen window
Touching her heavy hair.
I say "Don't be absurd,
You're not marooned,
Everyone knows and loves you."
She's nodding in black despair.

Looking out the window,
Gazing past the sails all furled,
Swaying slow in sorrow,
Looking for the freedom
At the end of the world.

Voyagers' songs see far.
The high notes ring,
Keening the hope, "Tomorrow,"
Gentling the past time closed.
She lilts the age-old airs.
Her true voice sings
Of love always giv'n, not borrowed;
Of giving she freely chose.

Her memory haunts the waters,
Sailor become,
Fairing in strangers' kingdoms,
Rowing in effortless whorls.
She is no one's daughter,
Nobody's son.
Easy to love, in freedom,
The ocean at the end of the world.

I wrote this after Don M left me, shortly before our intended wedding day in September 1962. I was in a kind of mourning the whole time I was dating Charlie F, which was the rest of my carefree college years. I graduated after I married Jim DeWitt in November of 1964, but in addition to taking classes I was also working full time at the U of Louisville Library, and those days were not at all carefree for me, as I *was supporting a husband who would not sing with me as we did so well, finish his last quarter at Speed School, or hold a job. I was making $1.00 per hour that year, and we barely paid our bills.*

Old Lucas Lane

(Chorus) Old Lucas Lane,
It's got no place but it's got a name.
Just goes to show that
Even to the hopeless, dear hope came.

I've got a friend who expects it will rain, always counting up his woes.
Every new day offers new pain. Seeds of sorrow are what he sows.
Talk and talk about yesterday, all the good things left to say;
Full of fear about tomorrow, never noticing today.
I'm a little puzzled, because today is full of sunlight.
But for the one who wills it so, it will always be dead of night

Chorus

One spring day, I saw a street sign; its name was Old Lucas Lane.
It's become trackless in the meantime, but the signpost does remain.
There's no walking on Old Lucas Lane. The road has disappeared.
What enchantment did pertain, what mistaken doubt or pain?
I wonder who lived on what's now a clover field.
Does anyone have memories sweet? Is there laughter deep concealed?

Chorus

Old Lucas Lane teaches me to hope, even though it's unseen.
When kindred fail to hear a cry for help I remember Lucas Lane.
Like a tree that the big ax felled, but it springs up all anew,
By Thy Son, see hope fulfilled. Your children You will fill.
Give me grace to name Hope, the desert's flower.
Come! Bloom inside my heart. Hide me in Your bower.

I wrote this on July 21 in that horrendous summer of 1984. We had moved to Camelot, which Don had brilliantly found and purchased, on April 4ᵗʰ. It was and is a wonderful old bungalow, not large, like a mansion, but adequate for us three and filled with light from over fifty three-by-six-foot windows.

However, when we moved here Don's mentality completely snapped, seemingly overnight. Before this, his state was distinctly odd for him.

Now he became dysfunctional. He could not eat. He doubted his ability to work as a pilot and always called in sick rather than work, although he had made 100% on a test flight he took at that time. It was utterly bewildering to me.

And Don had thoroughly trained me to do nothing without him. He wanted me in the same room with him; period, when he was at home, and it had been this way for a decade and more. Now, if I were to accomplish anything, I needed to do that on my own. My health was failing, with rheumatoid and organic symptoms constantly a challenge, and I focused on keeping up the exercise regimen those of Ra had requested I do, and continuing to serve with L/L Research. I tried and tried to help Don, but nothing I did or said made any difference. I felt that it was the failure of a lifetime for me, and I was constantly tempted to despair.

Along my walking route was a street sign, "Old Lucas Lane". It apparently had been a road but was now a field off Lucas Lane. Its appearance inspired these poetic thoughts.

On the Wings of a Song

On the wings of a song fly all my prayers to You.
I can open to being true my whole life long.
May my heart never cease in your songs to increase
On the wings, On the wings of a song

(Chorus) I receive His sweet peace
On the wings of a song.

There's a world that we see—or we think we see—with our eyes.
There's another we need to fully realize.
There's no need to compromise. Lift your voice unto Paradise
On the wings, on the wings of a song.

Chorus

Icarus tried for the sun with feathers and glue.
May we always remember our way to You
Lies in our reaching and seeking and being for you
On the wings, on the wings of a song.

Chorus

I wrote this August 4, 1991, in the most difficult days of my organic illness, just months before I had half my transverse colon removed. So often the brightest moments of inspiration come during hard times like this, for me anyway. It is always such a blessing when I am taken away by a mystical state... on the wings of a song.

The Pain of Living

(Chorus) The pain is in me, cold and still, the pain of living.
Needle-like, the drops, like rain, are shrill and unforgiving
It's the pain of living.

Hear that bird, singing out your front door?
What makes him sing so sweetly?
Is he in pain, or is it hunger,
Or does he feel at peace completely,
Just singing to fill my heart
Out of some God-given, instinctual art?

Chorus

Oh Lord, I feel the pain today,
The pain of living.
But how do I sing, Lord, and how do I pray
When I have no words to say,
And empty and lost is my heart,
And vain as my hope is my art?
But I'm thirsting for more, ever more of you.

Chorus

Footsteps echo on an empty street.
The buildings, are empty, their windows wood.
The wall river dust, gone gently to sleep
Is the hobo all wrapped up in his cloak,
His song hushed and resting apart
Like a bird all asleep in the nest of his heart.

Chorus

The pain is in me, the hobo wakes.
I don't remember just how to play,
But I offer to you, Lord, what music I make,
Be it ragtime or jazz time or blues that I play.
Lord, please, touch the pain in my heart.
Let me never think we are ever apart.

Chorus

I wrote this for the story and song project, The Journey, *which I did with my brother, Tommy, around 1978. I wrote the story and the words to most of the songs and Tommy put the music to words. We recorded our tape for the Christmas present to our parents in the basement of St. Mark's Episcopal Church on an out-of-shape tape recorder and I sang flat as a flitter that day. However we recorded the song again, although not the story, for the CD of the same name, which we recorded the next spring, in April.*

Set Free

Like a sailor on the land with the water beckoning so close at
hand,
Yet the sailor home he stays 'cause his ship was sunk and he must
earn his pay.
That's the way my mind so often feels as I spin my mental wheels
Then suddenly my mind is freed and it's roaming far at sea.

(Chorus) And then I praise the mystery
And welcome the epiphany
That tells me my life will be
Set free

When I was a little kid and my mama called, well, I just ran and
hid.
Now I'm over twenty one. Duty calls me. Hello gray skies, good-
bye sun!
Now, I know it's just a platitude but when I can calm my mind,
Then my life is just an attitude. That's the truth of what I find

Chorus

All of us are looking for all the freedom that we think life has in
store,
Making money if we're poor, getting smarter if we never knew the
score.
But the freedom is inside our heads when we stop the chasing
after.
As our thoughts to living live are led and there's laughter in the
rafters,

Chorus

This was part of the story-and-songs work I wrote, called The
Journey. *I remember working on this while I was still on Douglass
Boulevard, so I must have written it around 1979. Tommy's setting
for this is one of his very best. He set all the songs to music for me.*

Later on, I went to D.C. to record The Journey *with Tom and
worked at Dusk and Dawn studio with him, singing my parts on to
tape, while Mom accompanied us.*

Sister Pain

Hello, Sister Pain.
I thought to leave you when I slept,
But now the dawn's just crept
Into my eyes, and you remain,
My Sister Pain

(Chorus) Come, Holy Spirit, fill me with your glory,
Renew my life and show me how to tell Love's story.

O sharp, Sister Pain,
O jagged, ragged life I lead.
With you to guide, I fill my head,
To run Love's race, Love's Christ to gain,
My Sister Pain.

Chorus

Beloved Sister Pain
I offer hospitality,
A room, a meal, a cup of tea,
With gratitude for all I've gained
From Sister Pain.

Chorus

I wrote this on March 17, 1991, during a very difficult time. My health was at a true nadir. Until the surgeons relieved me of half my transverse colon I was a sick puppy indeed, unable even to breathe without significant pain, and bed-bound by arthritic crystallization so severe that my shoulders were frozen. I was unable to dress or care for myself, or eve to sit fully upright. After the colon operation, I went to pain management training and regained a good deal of my ability to use my shoulders and arms, and happily returned—after very hard work—to a vertical life. It was a wonderful change.

A Sorrowful Sun

A sorrowful sun creeps over the horizon
And looks down upon a hospital bed.
Most of the soldiers are dead or are dying
And few are around to repeat what you've said,
That—

We're winning, we're winning,
Winning the battle, not stopping to cry,
For the war is important and God's on our side,
Yes, we're winning.

Down in the market a young woman's shopping,
A babe in her stroller, a bag in her arms
A man on a skateboard, he stops and he asks her,
Please, where is your husband?" She says, "He's at war."
But—

Chorus

Then Jesus gets off of his skateboard and tells her,
"My sister, your husband has safely returned."
"No," says the woman, rocking the stroller,
"His body is here but his mind has been burned."
But—

Chorus

Now they cried together, the women and Jesus,
'Cause Jesus, he loves and he's been known to cry.
"What shall I do for my people," he asked her,
Gets back on his skateboard, rides back to the sky.
And—

Chorus

"Father," said Jesus, "I'm down on my knees
And I ask for your wisdom, I ask for your heart.
How can they say that you're on their side;
That God's love is tearing this planet apart?

They're not winning, not winning
Let them stop fighting, please let them start loving
For love is important, and God's on its side.
Then we're winning! Only then, we're winning.

The first verse and the Chorus to this song were written by Jim DeWitt, my first husband, sometime in the years preceding my meeting him in 1962. The rest of the verses are written by me. DeWitt never sang this song. I finished the writing for the song-story I did with my brother, Tommy, This is The Day.

Star Song

I want to be a star in your diadem.
I want to be a crystal of your mind.
Without your saving Spirit I am glass, I am glass.
Touch me with your heart that I may shine.

(Chorus) Soft summer country air, a wooden swing and my guitar.
Look at the fireflies
Oh, what a candle-glow! Don't miss the midnight show.
But don't mistake the lightning bugs for stars!

Gossamer evening my love hovering,
Caressing mist across the valley moving,
Water heard but never seen, fog bells at midnight keen
Wind, blow me where I must be roving.

Chorus

Nature's sweet caresses coax morning out of sleep.
Welcome as a promise comes the dawn.
Times cannot be stored away. Just this moment let me pray,
Let me always be Your very own.

Chorus

*On the manuscript it is noted that the words came through me on July
30, 1982, but I do not remember writing it. I can only guess that it
was one of those poems that flowed and flowered through me as I was
tuned to the devotion that flows through creation like an eternal
melody.*

Thank You

Down comes the rain
And out comes the sun
And another cycle of life is begun.
Down comes the dark
And up pops the light,
There are a thousand beauties to bless before night.

You can't say, "Thank you," enough times
Especially when going through rough times.

Thank you, praise you, bless you Lord.
Thank you for cycles.
Thank you for change.
Thank you for losses.
Thank you for gains.

It's all the same.
It's all so fine.
We thank you, Lord
All the time—
All of the circular time!

*I do not recall when I wrote this. It was probably in the 1990s.
Looking at the energy of it, I would guess it came to me on a walk—I
used to walk every day, for decades. I had to stop doing that around
2005, when my right foot started having stress fractures because of the
walking.*

Thanks for the Incarnation

O, glorious coins! O, blessed mint,
Our incarnations, heaven-sent.
From Thee we come, our spirits high.
Thy love to Him! Thy faith ever by.

(Chorus) Oh lord, the Lord of space and time
Our humble thanks to thee in rhyme.

Oh happy childhood, full of days
Of summer's incense, blossom-raised,
Of learning full, of family dear,
Of finding what we care to hear.

Chorus

Oh sweet our youth, that magic time
Of talk, of puzzling most sublime,
Of hungry nature, human need,
Of wisdom's discipline the seed

Chorus

Oh, fallow fields of middle age,
Of time when we all set our stage,
Of action, vision-seeker's quest,
Of fuller oneness with the Guest

Chorus

Oh, fine the time of harvest-home,
Of knowing that our work is done,
Of looking far and being free
At last to lose ourselves in Thee.

Chorus

I do not recall writing this. It sounds like me as a writer in the seventies or early eighties.

There's a Ribbon of Road

There's a ribbon of road a-winding
Before us all the time
On the way, there are crossroads
Of our heart, the truth, the rhymes.

(Chorus) Adore! Attend!
Hear! Remember!

We walk through this world unheeding
Of the rhythms of our souls
Forgetting and letting the earth-world
Remain real and our souls un-whole

Chorus

The tenor of this poem seems to me to fit it into my work in the 1990's.

Three A.M.

This is the hour when day is sleeping,
One small watchman vigil keeping.
Thank you, Lord, for being here with me.

The darkness rolls; its coils are binding,
Hopes and fears the night-time blinding.
Thank you, Lord for being here with me.

(Chorus) There is no light except inside.
May I crawl in with You?
Guardian angel of the night,
I know I'll be all right, with You.

Talking with You is blest salvation.
Freezing drunks in railway stations.
Thank You, Lord, for being there with them.

(Bridge 1) You can depend on me to depend on You.
When darksome dreams are in me, Your light illumines me.
Take my blinded eyes in Your gentle hands.
With sunrise my soul will understand.
And now, to rest in Thee,
And now, all praise to Thee.

This is the hour when love leaves footprints.
Cover me with love's sweet incense.
Thank You, Lord, for being here with me.

Chorus

(Bridge 2) The soul who calls on Thee may rest in a bed of lavender.
My soul, though lost to sleep, is filled full with Your provender.
If you're praying at three a.m., pray for light and it will come,
Blinding your eyes at three a.m. with bright, sweet thoughts of him.
And now, to joy in Thee—and watch the darkness flee.
Come, abide with Me at three a.m.
Soft and sweet at three a.m.

As sometimes happens, I do not remember writing this. It must have unrolled during sleep.

Transparent to Eternity

Starlight, remember me. The rain is pouring in,
Pouring out the tears of summer's end:
Roaring, weeping slaughter of the light.

(Chorus) I am nothing. Life runs through me,
So transparent
To eternity.

Blossoms barely born, remember all my dreams.
Waning moonlight, touch me with your tender beams.
Keep me, hold me, give me perfect peace this night.

Chorus

(Bridge) Please keep me in your mighty focus.
Remember me. Come to me.

Stars shining down, I need you tonight.
Blossoms, barely born, pale in silvery light
Promising to bloom in tomorrow's golden sight.

Chorus

I wrote this on July 10, 1991, although from the emotions carried therein I would have guessed it was a poem from college days. One word that strikes a chord, though, is "transparent". I recall feeling so ill, so weary and exhausted with it, that I felt transparent, as if all color had been leached away and I was living in moonlight.

The Tree of Life

Man was born within a garden,
Full of truth and free of strife.
In the garden stands a warden.
Prophets call it the tree of life.

Here's my friend with his hand on the latch
He shrugs his shoulders, drops the match
And his life is on fire, consumed like the light
Of the tree of life, of the tree of life.

Tree of life, your roots in heaven
Sweet seeds of eternity
Evergreens, your shade, like leaven,
Give us truth so light and free

Black old woman, rags for shoes
Wonder what she has to lose
Christmas day, she fights for the tree of life
For the tree of life.

(Bridge) Why do I want to say these things?
Why do I have this song to sing?
I'm yearning to stop the burning
Of the tree of life.
Of the tree of life

The body of the tree is man:
The sun his center;
Great his plan
His branches male and female be
Together in strength and harmony.

I wrote this in about 1986, I wrote this a part of a songs and story collection called This Is the Day.

Unseen Friends

They seem to flicker in the foggy mist,
Touching gently as a love's first kiss,
But like the lighthouse shining full onshore,
Though perceived as small, their strength is more,
My shining, unseen friends.

(Chorus) "For if we live, we live in Christ,
And if we die, we die in Christ,
So, whether we live or whether we die,
We are in Christ,
And Christ is in us. "[2]

I might live long, or maybe death is near.
But I take heart, and feel no chilling fear.
The hearts of all my dear companions shine
Serenely all around me. Peace is mine.
My strength is unseen friends.

Chorus

Bridge that goes on forever: is it by prayer
Created or magicked out of sheer midair?
Does faith create the span 'twixt heart and sense?
These seeming strangers, my beloved friends?
Thank you, my unseen friends.

Chorus

This was written on March 18, 1982, when I was struggling to offer myself for being channel for the Ra sessions. I had undiagnosed organic problems, and by severe rheumatoid symptoms which kept me challenged. Don especially was concerned that I might die. I recall being endlessly grateful for these unseen friends and for their very real comfort.

---

[2] This Chorus is a paraphrasing of Romans 14:8: "For whether we live, we live unto the Lord; and whether we die, we die unto the Lord: whether we live therefore, or die, we are the Lord's."

The original typescript bears the notation, "Dedicated to Tot and Marion, whom I "saw" first. They helped me see the millions of others."

Vision

The Master called me to the woods
And I to Him would go,
And dance with lilies for my veil
And bow my head down low.
Shy, mid daisies, up I looked
His shining face upon.
His blazing eyes looked down at me,
He whispered, "You have come."

"My Master, I would die for You,
Or labor night and day,
So you may see how easily
This order I obey.
These are the woods where oft I walk.
These ferny paths are mine.
How pleasant, then, to walk with You
This way, by Your design."

The Master stood and walked my way,
And motioned me to rise.
"You see in me such quality
As I would not surmise
To be mixed in My common clay,
For I am such as you.
Wherefore do you then find your way
To see My angel hue?"

I rose and stood, so proud and tall
To stand near such a man.
"My Master, there's a universe
Which You can deftly scan
Which makes the world of such as I
A pitiable plan.
Your heart is great; it never lacks
The strength to reach and span

The distances 'twixt You and me,
'Twixt You and everyone.
Oh, Master, Your world's like the day,
And You, Lord, are my sun.
What wonder then that willingly

I came this way for you?
To go where you are not; that is
What would be hard to do.

I remember writing this just after my wedding to Jim DeWitt at Thanksgiving, 1964. My little world had fallen apart. My first husband refused the singing which had brought us together. Indeed, I rarely saw him. But the Master of my life was right there, and I followed Him with joy.

Waves

Wave upon wave, moment by moment,
I am a bubble, Lord, make me the sea.
Tide after tide, time after time,
Lord, I surrender. Hide me in Thee.

(Chorus) I cling to Thee. I sing to Thee.
Open my heart, Beloved, to Thee

I never thought I had a vagabond heart,
I was the child who stayed at home.
Yet I've found myself a Prodigal Son.
Was it wonderful to roam?

Chorus

Fear after fear, sin upon sinning,
I am a pilgrim, Lord, walking in Thee:
Walking forever, yet never moving,
I am a bubble, Lord. Make me the sea.

Chorus

*I studied Paramahansa Yogananda's writings in the seventies and was
especially entranced with his little spiritual song, "I am a Bubble".
Stealing this phrase shamelessly from the great teacher, I wrote this
poem during Jim's and my Pawley's Island vacation in 1993..*

Web of Love

I've been on the trail a long time. Evening's coming on,
Help is on its way, I understand.
If romance is gone, well, that's a crime, bow my head on down,
But raise it up again 'cause I'm a man.

(Chorus) 'Cause I'm a man who believes that my friends are on
their way.
And I'm a man who hopes to see the light that shines that day.
I feel the web of love touching round me and above.
Oh I feel the web of love.

The trail passed through the silver mountains, berries wet with
dew,
Dawn afire with spikes of red and white.
Drinking from the crystal fountains, looking at the view,
I hope I meet my friends before I die.

(Bridge) Love never leaves us. It's we who are away.
Open up your heart and feel the web of love today.

Chorus

Coming to the desert now, country strange to me.
I don't know the names of what I'm seeing.
It's cold at night but there's no snow. Visions pale I see.
I think they are the shadows of my being

Chorus

This poem was one used in the song-and-story The Journey. *I wrote
the poetry for the piece and the story and Tommy put the poetry to
music. We sang this song together.*

Where Is My Heaven?

(Chorus) Tell me where is my heaven?
What I hear is, it's so fine to see.
It's so wonderful to be there.

Sometimes I just have to ask the question, like, was it last week
I saw in a show about the human race,
The makers of the movie, they had found us
Raising kids and building houses.
Getting fat and oh so lazy, pushing up the daisies.

Chorus

Stopping by a church last week, I questioned,
"Hey, tell me, preacher, where is heaven, 'cause I'm searching oh,
so hard?"
He just smiled and printed vaguely upward,
Touched my head with holy water,
Asked me back to come and seek one day every week.

Chorus

When I asked a Hare Krishna, "Where is heaven?" He said,
"Mister,
Hare, hare, give me money, make me hum".
Then I felt a glow, the sun was shining,
Closed my eyes and God was smiling
And I knew where heaven is—
All around and in it is.

Chorus

Tommy wrote music for this poem and it is included in a song-and-story which I wrote and for which Tommy created the music. We recorded it on tape for our parents' Christmas gift around 1994. We had wonderful fun doing these creations together, with both of us singing and reading back and forth in the stories.

Why Do We Pass It By?

Cold winds following like barking dogs.
All the grass is brown and gray.
Walking along the street in a fog.
Who would notice one silent bird
On such a mean day?
Tiny creature, feathers small, balancing against the wind
Just because he didn't sing, I missed perfection again.

(Chorus) Oh why do we pass it by?
How can we let it go?
When the truth is so nearby
Why do we pass it by?

Turning the corner on a spring and flower day,
A man in a sweatshirt, ripped and blue,
Looks at me. I avoid his gaze.
He slouches over, "Lady, I love you.
Lady, I really love you."
Fragile man with his clothes all torn—
Is this how Jesus looks if it's now He was born?

Chorus

See the little black kids on the big TV
And the "Send your donations to …
Birds of paradise in bones, page twenty-two."
Other people's hunger doesn't touch you—
You slide on through.
News of the world has a hollow ring.
When did it cease to mean anything?

I recall publishing this in my church's United Thank Offering letter, when I was UTO officer there in the mid-nineties. So that's the era during which I wrote it. Naturally, the inspiration was birds on a wire in winter. For a change, I remember the moment with clarity, and the realization of how much beauty we routinely miss still moves me.

Wings

(Chorus) I put my faith in wings.
I'm like the empty mail tray,
Full of nothing every day,
Until tomorrow brings me
Messages and wings.

They said that man would never fly
While the bumblebee just smiled,
Leonardo sketched busily,
As the bees plumbed clover's guiles
They used to say the earth was flat
Till Magellan's "wild surmise",
People tell me this and that,
If they're saying no, they're liars

Chorus

Under the shadow of his opinions
Man sees the dominions of His promised land,
Where kindliness and graciousness
Carve spaciousness of mind,
Glowing pearls from grains of sand;
Solid souls from mortal dust;
Children in His hands.

Chorus

The water closes over me,
Human lungs in need of air,
Promises the eyes can't see
False illusions hard to bear
But every time life knocks me down,
Patience pulls me out to sea.

(Bridge) There we fly so freely!

Chorus

*I wrote this on July 25, 1984,, but this is a constant part of my nature
and my faith. I could have written it any time these last fifty years!*

CHRISTIAN POETRY
AND SONGS

All I Discover

It's only when I lose myself
That I find myself in You,
Only when I die away
Like the ending of the day.
It's only when I yield my will
That I'm still enough to know
What it is you'd have me do,
What new land holds promise true,

For I find myself in you.
You are my explanation.
I lose myself in you.
You do my exploration.
And all I discover praises you.

It's only when I yield my shape
And my limits to the cave,
Only when I am no more
In any sense save to adore,
Only when I utterly die
And sink into the grave
That angels come with trumpet's tone
To roll away the light-struck stone.

And all I discover praises You
All I discover praises You.

I wrote this at Calvary Episcopal Church during a Quiet Day that was held in Advent on December 13, 1986. As I sat in the congregation, musing on a meditation read from the pulpit, these words came to me. My brother, Tommy, put this song to music but it has not been recorded. Stapled to the poem is a hymn, not of my writing, that we sang together:

Father, we adore You. Lay our lives before You. How we love You. Jesus, we adore You. Lay our lives before You. How we love You. Spirit, we adore You. Lay our lives before You. How we love You. Shepherd, we adore You. Lay our lives before You. How we love You.

Ambassador in Chains

To love and mourn is bread and meat
To me, who keeps the widow's watch
And gazes long at crying seas
As if my eyes could dead men fetch—
As if my eyes could see.

(Chorus) Ambassador, apostle of the Holy One of Israel,
Speaking through tears, I cannot witness well,
And Spirit, I am praying to You.

When one fine creature's found on Earth,
The light about him shines so bright
That when his soul gains heaven's birth,
The hole he leaves just swallows light
So that it seems midnight.

Chorus

I'll take the helmet of salvation;
Take in peace the suffering, too.
That is part of God's creation.
I must pray before I do.
Oh, sweet mystery, pull me through.

I wrote this in the middle of a sleepless night in September 2, 1985, after Don Elkins died. For the next several years I was caught up in the grief I felt at his passing. It felt as though the person I was then had died as well as he. It was only slowly that I came to feel reborn into a new life, which I came to feel was the time to live the Law of One.

Angels

(Chorus) O, to have faith!
O, to believe!
O, to feel grace!
And peace to receive!

Sometimes I feel like I'm caught on the stairs,
The first floor ugly and the second one fair,
And I want to see the air is full of angels!
The daily business has got to be done
The chores laid to rest and the day's race won
And I want to see the Son of Man and the angels.

Chorus

(Bridge) "Truly, truly, you'll see greater things than these!
You will see the heavens opened,
And the angels of God ascending and descending
Upon the Son of Man."[3]

I saw on television just the other night that
The Russians are coming and the world's not right,
And I want to have the sight to see the angels.
Nathanael said, "Can anything good
Come out of a hick town's worker in wood?"
And I want to see, if I only could, the angels.

(Coda) You know that I've been looking, for a really long time.
Inside, in scripture, in music and rhyme
And I can say, "Keep on! I've seen the angels."

This was written around on January 25, 1982, at a time when I typically would not sleep much during the night because of the discomfort of rheumatoid disease aggravated by serious illness internally. This discomfort went on for many years, until half my transverse colon was removed in January, 1992, and then I rehabilitated some of the rheumatoid problems in my back and shoulders. Until that occurred, I was prone to severe stomach and back spasms. However, paradoxically, during those sleepless nights I was

---

3 John 1:51.

often taken into mystical states where I could "see" some of the spiritual beauty for which I longed.

Behold! The Virgin Is with Child!

"Behold, the Virgin is with child,
And she shall bear a son,"
Said God to Ahaz. Yet the wild
Man, Rezin, and the son
Of Remaliah fights; is felled.
Our God-With-Us, Immanuel,
Has come to the stable.

(Chorus) Come to the stable!
Come to the Child so helpless.
Come if you are able!

(Bridge) We are defined by the birth of Jesus.

"Behold, I send my messenger,
He goes before your face,
Crying in the wilderness
The wellborn words of grace".
Thus John calls us through time and space,
To make our pathway neat and straight.
Come to the stable!

Chorus

"Behold from this time all the folk
Of ages shall call me blessed,"
Says Mary, virgin, in the yoke
Of exaltations dressed.
"For the Mighty One has done
Great things for me," Come, everyone,
Come to the stable.

Chorus

Bridge 2 He has raised up a cradle in the desert of our hearts,
We must keep our word to show all mercy for our part.
Mercy toward our hearts so deep,
And His covenant to keep.

"Behold, the Word is flesh, and dwells
Among us," says the Witness,
"And now behold His glory swells.
Light swallows all the darkness.

The Law was given by Moses' ruth,
But Jesus comes in grace and truth!
Come to the stable.

(Coda) Oh, I confess, nor ever deny.
"Come to the stable", is my cry.
Come to the stable.

This poem was written on Christmas Day, 1990. I was at that time setting up the Communion table and taking it down for a Tuesday morning Bible Study class at Calvary Church, and often would ponder the verses studied—these are from Isaiah—long after the class was over and I had gone home. I have very fond memories of working in the Sacristy with the blessed objects, paten, chalice, all the accoutrement of Holy Eucharist in the Episcopal Church, and feeling very blessed by my immersion in sacred things.

Blessed

Gently rein me in.
Softly let me cry.
From the sin within,
Keep me 'til I die.

Blessed are the poor in spirit.
God will wipe each tear from their eyes.

Break my foolish dreams,
When I would hold sway
With my human schemes.
Wash them all away

Blessed are the meek in spirit.
God will wipe each tear from their eyes

Heat me in the flame!
Temper me with fire!
Hone me with your Name!
Teach me Your desire.

Blessed are the poor in spirit.
God will wipe each tear from their eyes.

Oh, Lamb, be my shepherd.
Guide me to Thy springs
Of living waters.
Bathe me as I sing.

Blessed are the merciful.
God will wipe each tear from their eyes.

This poem was written sometime in the 1990s, when I was involved with the midweek bible study and communion services at Calvary. Clearly I was pondering the Beatitudes.

Blessings

You touched me, Lord. Your sleeve brushed mine
At that long table, offering bread.
I took the bread made so divine.
For then, for now, all souls are fed.

Your eyes were tired, my gentle teacher,
As You gave the wine to me.
"Take this wine," you told all seekers,
"'Tis My blood I shed for thee."

(Chorus) We are here in the fullness
Of the blessing of the gospel of Christ.[4]
We are here in the fullness
Of the blessing of God the Father.

I am caught in this sad moment.
Puzzled, yet I shall obey,
As you bring me to Your presence
At this feast, this bliss, today.

Coda You are my strength, you are my song
And my salvation all the day long.
I shall not die, but I shall live,
And tell of the feast,
And tell of this moment,
Tell of the works of the Lord!

I wrote this song for the songs-and-story work, The Journey. *The date was somewhere around 1979. Tommy liked the song and still sings it at his gigs in Christian coffeehouses ad concerts.*

---

[4] Romans 15:29: "And I am sure that, when I come unto you, I shall come in the fullness of the blessing of the gospel of Christ."

The Body of Christ

Sounds of home around me crowd in plentiful bouquet.
In the garden earth is plowed, the sky cloudless and gay.
Sounds within my mind proclaim a day of bitter gray,
Where good and lovely things are maimed and lightless is the day.

(Chorus) The body of Christ; the bread of life.
The blood of Christ; the cup of salvation.[5]

What feast of fear so folly-full; what drink of wormwood eat
Instead of Your sweet feast? O Jesus, I can't hear.
O, speak to me, and please speak clear. Reach me, teach me, hold
    me near,
O mild, O blessed one, most dear, in Thy triumph I feast.

(Bridge) "Fear not, I am with Thee."
I'm listening, I'm listening.
The laws of love are perfect.
I'm listening, I'm listening.
Keep me from presumption. Lay for my consumption
A feast of Body and of Blood—
And ears to listen and to hear.

Chorus

In my heart I'm listening, though faint Thy words; unclear;
Butterfly still glistening; birth cocoon so near.
Fill my ear with Your dear Word; grant me grace to hear.
Fed with His body, washed in His blood—saving Words of cheer.

Chorus

I wrote this on March 10, 1985. I can recall nothing about its writing and assume it was one of those poems that flowed through me when I was worshiping.

---

[5] These phrases are part of the Rite of Holy Eucharist in the Episcopal Church.

Day of Darkness

Seems the days get longer when you're traveling.
Seems the first robin's much harder to see.
Seems my heart is tempted to feel kind of down.
Seems my outside doesn't match the inside "me".
But stop! The Moore's forsythia is yellow.
Spring must have stopped here after all.
And I'm not so far—not so very far
From my home.

(Chorus) Blow the trumpet in Zion!
Sound a warning on my holy mountain![6]
Day of clouds, Day of darkness.
I'm coming, Lord, running
To your home.

Once I prayed and wept, but no one saw me.
Once I turned to truth from all the lies.
Once my left forgot about my right hand.
Once a Savior taught with parables wise.
Oh, yes! The man who fasts need not be dismal,
For the end of the fasting is the feast!
And we have all, who have the very least.
We are home.

(Bridge) Jesus, I'm on this journey with you—
I who am Good Friday's dust and dreams
I mean to say—in every way—
I see you.
I love you.
I rise with you
To my home.

I believe I wrote this around 1994. I do not recall anything about it except being moved by reading Joel's prophecies in the Bible.

---

6 Joel 2:1: "Blow ye the trumpet in Zion, and sound an alarm in my holy mountain: let all the inhabitants of the land tremble: for the day of the Lord cometh, for [it is] nigh at hand."

How We Thirst

Is it wise to tag along
On the coattails of destruction?
How much do we want to touch
Heart's grief and fell destruction?
I hear the voice of Micah say,
When I ask for his instruction,
"Do justly.
Love mercy.
Walk humbly with your God."[7]

Are we're smart to share what we are
When to speak is seen as treason?
What do we have the heart to say
When the truth is not in season?
With my heart at peace, I find an ease
In faith's undaunted reasons.
"Do justly.
Love mercy.
Walk humbly with your God."

There is no date on this poem. My guess would be that I was in Bible study classes when I was inspired by Micah's words, which would put this as written sometime in the mid-1990s.

---

[7] These words are a paraphrase of Micah 6:8, "He hath shewed thee, O man, what is good; and what doth the LORD require of thee, but to do justly, and to love mercy, and to walk humbly with thy God?"

Don't Do It Twice

Walking on the path of life with my suitcase in my hand.
Carrying all my memories and the things I think I understand
The first thing that I know for sure is we all lead a sinner's life
The second thing I think I know is: Don't repeat the same sin twice.

(Chorus) Don't do it twice. Don't do it twice.
For God is merciful but just—
Don't do it twice, now. Don't do it twice.
That's my advice.

If we each are temples of the light, we show the glory of his Life.
If the water of our life runs dry, there's something we're not doing right.
So just sit you down in the temple, and pray for crystal eyes.
Falsehoods are written in the Book of Life, so don't repeat the same sin twice.

Chorus

"Peace I leave with you," He said, *"Peace I give to you.*
Let not your hearts be troubled,
Neither let them be afraid."[8]
Listen to the Counselor's voice.
And don't repeat the same sin twice!

At Lystra, Paul was misnamed Hermes; Barnabas, they called Zeus
Paul said, "Wait, we are men like you, and that's the God's own truth!"[9]
Now God allowed the nations to walk in their own ways,
Filled your hearts with gladness. But don't forget today.

Chorus

I do not recall writing this, but it probably comes from the mid-nineties. That was my Bible Study period.

---

[8] John 14:27, "Peace I leave with you, my peace I give unto you: not as the world giveth, give I unto you. Let not your heart be troubled, neither let it be afraid."

[9] The story is told by Paul in Acts, Chapter 14.

Don't Gain on the Train

Jacob had the dearest dear
Don't gain on the train.
Wanted her for seven years.
It'll come round again.
When he went, his love to gain
Don't gain on the train.
Another seven years of pain.
It'll come round again.

(Chorus) There isn't any gaining on the train
When you have to stop at the crossing.
Till the track is clear again.
Wait it out. Keep your lamp trimmed neat
Work it out with help from the Mercy Seat.

Virgins wise, they trimmed their wicks.
Don't gain on the train.
Every moment ready for the midnight tick.
It'll come round again.
The foolish virgins lost their lights.
Don't gain on the train.
Midnight comes and they have no light.
It'll come round again.

Chorus

I wrote this on March 30, 1985, in the midst of the Ra contact sessions.

Earthen Vessels

(For Roman, who asked.)

If Jesus were a tax collector,
How would He be?
Christ as an IRS Director –
What would we see?
I'd hope to get Him on an audit
If I were an honest person,
But if I'd tried tax fraud, it's
Him I'd fear, and that's for certain.
He was human, just like you and me.

If Jesus were a carpenter –
Historically—that's He.
We put Jesus so far from us,
How can we see?
Pursue the mind of Christ the King:
He takes us to a simple cave
Of heart and bone and listening –
We have that same chapel, you and me.

We have treasure without measure
In this house of clay: CHRIST IN US today!
Thanks be to God. Praise be to God.
WE pray to you, Lord God, Who walked this sod.

Amen.

I remember writing this prayer-song on February 24, 1993. I was on a walk here around Camelot and had to stop in at a dentist's office at the corner of Evergreen and Hazelwood and beg some paper and a pen as I could not retain it for the walk home. It was pouring through too quickly.

Eli, Eli, Lama Sabachtani!

(Intro) Eli, Eli, lama sabachtani![10]
Where is the mercy?
Sometimes it's hard to trust in you.

It's hard to see my friend locking his chains,
Turning the key shut once again.
Does he need it? Can he use it?
Freedom's right within his grasp.
All he needs to do is ask.
Does he fear it? He's so near it.

(Chorus) Those who are planted in the house of the Lord
Shall flourish, shall flourish in the courts of our God—

I do it to myself, see a cloudy sky,
And drink up all the shadows bye and bye.
Do I need it? Can I use it?
Challenges sometimes run me down
And, by myself, I fall flat on the ground
What do I fear when I'm so near to God?

Chorus

Maybe one day before I'm all turned gray,
I'll have it figured out what it means to pay.
Oh, I need it. I can use it.
Sick, sad, hungry, yes, the world is flawed,
But when I am rested in the living Lord,
There is a feeling. There's healing.

Chorus

(Coda) Eli, Eli, lama sabachtani!
Sometimes it's easy to trust in You.

---

[10] "Eli, Eli lama sabachtani" occurs in the Bible (Matthew 27: 45-6) and means, "My God, my God, why hast Thou forsaken me?" It is said at the beginning of the Jewish funeral service, and it is conjectured that Jesus, when he cried this out before He died on the cross, was saying His own service.

This poem comes from my Bible Study period in the mid-nineties. I recall pondering the poignancy of Jesus' cry.

Faith, Sweet Hannah

"For not by might shall man prevail,"[11]
Our sister, Hannah, prayed.
And yet, as angels cry, does Baal
Cry war, and by obeyed
By tyrants and by presidents,
By high men and by low;
Yet god shall judge unto the ends
Of all the Earth below.

Faith, sweet Hannah, was your home.
Bless your spirit's either/or.
Prince of Peace, I beg you come!
Bring to naught unholy war.

Those who vie against the Lord
Shatter into dust,
While only peaceful folk afford
The Word that cannot rust.
Oh, armies, put your weapons down
And leave the heap of ashes,
For no one's holy like the Lord
And all things else shall pass us.

O, holy night
O, hear the angels singing.
O, night divine!
My spirit there is winging.

War now waits on desert sand,
And all the grief it brings,
While soft, without a human hand
Doth come the King of Kings.
I cry for my beloved Earth
And pray for war to cease,
While I count the hours until Your birth,
Beloved Prince of Peace.

---

[11] Hannah's prayers were powerful. In 1 Samuel 2:4, she prayed, "The bows of the mighty men are broken, and they that stumbled are girded with strength."

The pillars of the Earth are the Lord's
My heart lifts in joy to hear this Word.

I wrote this poem during my Bible Study period in the nineties, after the '92 tummy operation relieved me of half my transverse colon and I rehabilitated my frozen shoulders to regain a vertical life. I truly believe in the power of prayer, and I truly hope that war shall cease! The sentiments expressed in this poem are themes of my whole adult life.

Give in Faith Today

All Earth's folk are taught the same,
That when His hour came, He did pray,
"O, Father, glorify Thy name,"
And then the voice from heaven rang.

Now it is the moment sweet
When you may open wide
Your hand, and cast your grains of wheat
Upon the countryside

What gifts are there? O! Watch and pray,
And let the seeds come as they may,
For soon the earth will know your heart
If you but live in faith today

I cannot recall when this was written except that it was in the period around 1979, when my brother, Tommy, and I were actively creating songs together with my words and his music.

He Is There

(Chorus) The earth is Thy bread. The air is Thy wine.
We are the branches of Thy vine.

Close my eyes in sorrow, sit upon the shore.
Think not on tomorrow 'til today is sure.
Out to sea I'm taken, rudderless and tossed,
Desolate, forsaken, sight of land is lost

Chorus

Waters are a desert. Oceans have no ways.
Drowning in Gennesaret[12], faithless fall the days.
Breathe the salty water, sink down in despair.
Hark ye, sons and daughters! Even now, He's there.

Chorus

(Bridge) He is there! He is with us, Right this moment, He is there,
There for me, there for you, there for people everywhere.
He is there.

Jesus, be my rudder. Show Thy path to me.
Homeward sails the pilgrim, no more lost at sea.
Now You set my two feet firmly on the ground.
Thanks and praise be to Thee from the lost who's found.

Chorus

I wrote this for Tommy to put to music on February 15, 1985. However Tommy would not write music for me from this year until 2010, when he decided that my channeling did not preclude his working with me. During that interim Tommy tried his level best to persuade me to stop channeling. I finally cut off communication with him as this matter was very painful for me to endure. Tommy has quite a gift for rhetoric and I would not let myself say anything in self-defense. Finally he had a breakthrough and discovered that he could, indeed, go for the balance of his incarnation without mentioning the channeling again. Whew! All is well with us now.

---

[12] Gennesaret is an old name for the Sea of Galilee.

Heal Me Again

Once I came to you full of faith
Once I asked and I knew.
All that was old would be bathed away
All that was old would be new.

(Chorus) How I rejoiced! How I adored!
How I praised the risen Lord!
How I praised the risen Lord.

How sure I was that I was saved,
Safe from evil forever,
Far outside of a world that raved,
Armored from all ill whatever.

Chorus

(Bridge) How little we know when we're counting.
The smug are as poor as the doubting.
Only You—Only You—Only You.

Now I come to you, worn and lost.
My feet are tired as my queries.
The path I've walked is called "Don't count the cost,"
But Lord, legs and heart are so weary.

(Chorus) How to rejoice? How to adore?
How to praise You, risen Lord?
How to praise You, risen Lord?

The blind man at Bethsaida asked for his sight
And Jesus laid hands on his pain.
But one touch failed to put him to rights,
So Jesus touched him again

Chorus

Heal me again, Lord, O touch me again,
Open the beauty of life to me
Once I could see it, then lost, here I stand,
O, Jesus, heal me again!

(Chorus) And I rejoice and I adore
How I praise You, risen Lord!
How I praise You, risen Lord!

I wrote this as a song for Tommy and me to sing together when he had composed the music for it on April 23, 1986. It was never put to music. Tommy had decided not to work with me, as a matter of his faith. He was concerned that my being a channel was not something he could accept. Although we never created bad feelings between ourselves because of this difference of opinion, we did not see each other for a couple of years.

Then a miracle happened, and Tommy realized that he and I could have this difference between us without it being his responsibility to change my thinking. So I have hopes we shall work together again one fine day!

Hello Lord

Hello Lord, I'm calling long distance.
Thought I reach out and touch you today.
Seems like years since we sat down together
With the bread and the wine and the Way.
I'm as lazy as the moon, hiding from noon
In my dark room of perishing clay.

(Chorus) I've taken you for granted
Like a sweetheart been married too long.
But today, my heart is made new, and I come back to you,
Jesus, my Lord, for Your glory this song.

Please forgive me for forgetting to call you—
It's a lot harder thing than it seems.
First, I had to let go all my baggage,
Wake up from my renegade dreams,
Then I had to find a phone, scared and alone,
Playing no-show with tickets in my jeans.

(Chorus) Oh, hear the telephone sing to me,
Playing pianissimo, Lord.
Make me an instrument, Lord,
Make me an instrument of Thy peace.

(Bridge) There's a trick to calling You, Jesus.
Though the phone booths are placed all around,
The coins in the mind cannot find You,
Only the heart's wired for sound.
Dial 0 for Operator. Forget human nature.
By immeasurable grace we are found.

Chorus

*I wrote this for Tommy sometime in the eighties. He put it to music
and sings it when he concertizes.*

Home for the Holidays

(For Tommy.)

Children home from school,
Weather getting cool.
I'm going home for the holidays.
People full of buying,
Old year full of dying,
Everyone smiling in the holidays.

(Chorus) Home, what does it mean?
Is it where we were born?
Is it where we have been?
Or is it where we are on Christmas morn?

Jesus, infant child,
Mary, undefiled,
I'll come to you in the holidays.
Shepherds with their sheep,
Angel voices sweet
Lead me home to my heart's place.

Chorus

The stable is home
Where my spirit roams.
My soul, kneeling, comes near.
It is dark and cold
Yet I there would hold
To breathe, in the straw, heaven's air.

Chorus

*I wrote this poem for Tommy and me to sing on September 12, 1994,
but we never created it together—at least not yet!*

I Love Jesus

I love the healing power of Jesus' name.
I love the healing power of Jesus' name.
Even if you don't believe
Just to say it will relieve
The burden that you bear of stress and strain.

I love the saving seal of Jesus' name.
I love the saying seal of Jesus' name.
Even if you think protection
Doesn't live in that direction
Yet now the peace you feel is really real.

I love the living mind in Jesus' name.
I love the living mind in Jesus' name.
Just give him some time each day
When you meditate and pray,
Read and ponder, see how wondrous that He came.

I believe I wrote this in the late 1970s. I intended it as a song for Tommy and I to sing together. That did not happen, however.

I Love the Healing Power of Jesus' Name

I love the healing power of Jesus' name.
I love the healing power of Jesus' name.
Even if you don't believe,
Just to say it will relieve
The burden that you bear of stress and strain.

(Bridge) And He will, He will!
Try to deny it, but no way.
For you are filled
When you say His Name

(Chorus) Praise to thee, immortal Word!
Holds it love and healing touch.
Holds it blood and pain and cross.
Holds it One who died for us.

I love the saving seal of Jesus' name.
I love the saving seal of Jesus' name.
Even if you thought protection
Didn't live in that direction
You know the peace you feel is really real.

Chorus

I love the living mind in Jesus' name.
I love the living mind in Jesus' name.
Give him an hour a day
While you meditate and pray,
Read and ponder, see how yonder grows the Game.

Chorus

(Coda) Jesus, Jesus, Jesus, Amen.

I wrote this in the August of 1990. It is noted on the typescript that I "felt" the words in three quarter time. It really is a "feel good" song! I also jotted down a tune for the Chorus, but as I edited today, I just did not like it much, so am omitting it I hope that Tommy will do much better with the melody.

I Need You, Lord

Today, I rejoice that I am broken,
Spinning off the wheel of the world.
Now I am glad to feel forsaken,
For now I am ready for Your Word.

(Chorus) I need you, Lord,
So seed me, Lord,
That my empty heart
May never part
From fruitful harvest in You.

Today, I thank God I am a failure,
Dropping all the balls that fly my way.
See, how my heart is like a sailor,
Lost in rum and longing for sea-spray!

Chorus

(Bridge) God of power, God of might—
Fill my emptiness this night.
Lord of wholeness, Lord of One
Fill me with the risen Son.

Today, I reach out and say, "I'm sorry,"
And, God, You reach right back out to me.
Teach me, O Savior, to stay empty
That I may always have blest need of Thee.

Chorus

I wrote this April 24, 1986, during the long period after Don died in November, 1984 and before I rehabbed after my colonectomy in January 1992. It was a dark night of the soul for me. How merciful was the dawn!

I Shall Rejoice

Once I came to you full of faith.
One I asked and I knew.
All that was old would be bathed away.
All that came would be new.

(Chorus) How we rejoiced! How we adored!
How we praised the risen Lord!

How sure I was that I was saved,
Safe from evil forever,
Far outside of a world that raved,
Armored from all ill whatever.

(Chorus) How I rejoiced! How I adored!
How I praised the Risen Lord!

(Bridge) How little we know when we're counting.
The smug are as poor as the doubting.
Only You. Only You. Only You.

Now I come to you, worn and lost.
My feet are as tired as my queries.
The path I've walked is called, "Don't count the cost".
But, Lord, legs and heart are so weary.

(Chorus) How to rejoice? How to adore?
How do I praise You, Risen Lord?

The blind man at Bethsaida asked for his sight
And Jesus laid hands on his pain.
But one touch failed to put him to rights.
So Jesus touched him again.

(Chorus) How he rejoiced! How he adored!
How he praised the Risen Lord!

Heal me again, Lord, O touch me again,
Open Your beauty to me,
Once I could see it, now lost here I stand,
Help me to see You again!

(Chorus) And I shall rejoice! I shall adore!
I shall praise You, Risen Lord!

I probably wrote this in the eighties. I wrote it for Tommy and me to sing together but it was never put to music.

I Will Follow You

I will follow you wherever you may lead.
My life is in your hands. You know my every need.
Not waiting for tomorrow, only living for today.
Don't want to let Your opportunity slip away.

(Chorus) Away from you, life is cardboard.
Away from you, gone's the sun.
Away from you, I have no Lord.
I am yours, Beloved Son.

Now is full of you! This very moment's yours.
You surround me with Your gifts and souvenirs.
Let me forget my small self, the Spirit is what I need
Let me rest as Your Providence drops Its seeds.

Chorus

God on my left hand, God on my right
Above, below, without, within, dawning, noon and night.

I wrote this sometime in the eighties for Tommy and me to sing together. However we have not put it to music or performed it yet.

I'll Just Be There

So much pain, my brother,
Spreading out like a pool of water.
Where is the criminal mother
Who has left her daughter?

(Chorus) But I'll just be there
I'll always be there
Wherever people err
I'll just be there.

Shall I judge you, brother,
Making buildings in your mind?
Where is mercy for others?
When did you become less than kind?

Chorus

Sleep your trance, dance your dance.
Follow fancies, find romance.
When you're ready, wait for Me—
I'll just be there, waiting for thee.

Chorus

Have you heard my Father
Speaking in the wind and sea?
Listen, if you'd rather—
Learn from silence. And come to me.

Chorus

I would guess I wrote this in the early eighties. I do not recall writing it at all.

Jesus Is Cool

(Chorus) Now He says, "Love the Lord your God."—now, that's simple!
"And love one another. Groove on your brother.
Then He'd go on down the line, changing water into wine.
Man, Jesus is cool, Jesus is cool
He went to cool school, fool!
Jesus is cool

Hey, my friend, I hear you been thinking.
That Jesus is square.
And when you've been drinking
And feel yourself sinking,
You know that no one is there.
So you grab all the gusto that you can.
And you stand there, a big brave man.
Then the barroom closes and alone you stand,
Because you think the Lord's nowhere.
But Jesus is cool.

Chorus

See they teach you in our modern schools that Jesus ain't cool
'Cause this ancient honky, he rode on a donkey
Or, sometimes, a mule.
But if you'll wipe the dust right off that Holy Book,
And open it up and take a good look
You'll find Jesus' fish line has a hook
And he's ready to save us fools.
Cause Jesus is cool.

Chorus

I wrote this for the songs-and-story creation, The Journey, *which Tommy and I created for our parents' Christmas present in the mid- to late-eighties. This is not the complete version and I will try to find the missing verses. Tommy and I had a great time with this song!*

John, Son of Zechariah

(Chorus) Go out weeping.
Each tear becomes a seed.
And we shall reap them all with tears of joy.

John, son of Zechariah,
I come, weeping, come to you,
A thorn bush, repenting its thorns
Seeks, seeks, seeks to be born anew.

Chorus

Paul, partner in the Gospel,
Bound in prison, bound in chains—
Christ's love, so full in your heart.
Speaks, speaks, speaks to my soul again.

Chorus

(Bridge) Jesus, you lifted your head
From the hard cross of your sorrow
To speak of Paradise before tomorrow.

Come, everlasting mountains,
Be made level, be made low,
And the low plains, valleys of pain,
Rise, rise, rise; His glory show.

Chorus

Written on December 7, 1982, this is the result of my brooding over the life and fate of John the Baptist, Jesus' cousin and baptizer. He has always fascinated me because of his faith and devotion, humility and steadfastness. A man who eats locusts cannot be said to have an easy life, and John's simple acceptance of suffering at the simplest level of creature comforts always struck me as wonderfully powerful.

Joy in the Morning

She's been acting differently.
Doesn't care to say why.
Amethyst and gold and gently,
Leaves drift bye and bye.
It's been a dry, dry year.
The creek is low this fall.
Though the water's pure and clear,
The banks are very tall.

(Chorus) Those who go through a desolate valley
Will find it a place of springs.
Those who spend the night in sorrow
Will find joy in the morning.
Joy when the morning comes.

(Bridge) The rains will fall
The lake will rise.
Happiness always
Takes me by surprise.

Maybe she's holding burdens,
New country blues in her hands;
Back of her eyes a curtain
Hiding the promised land.
It's been a dry, dry year.
Her heart got caught in winter,
So the summer made her cry.
Whirlpool at the center of love's autumn eye.

Bridge

Chorus

I wrote this while studying the Bible with the Calvary Church Bible Study group on Tuesdays, in the mid-nineties. The reference is to Psalm 30, verse 5, "Weeping may last through the night, but joy comes with the morning."

The Lord Has Done Great Things

(Chorus) I want to jump up, reach out
Hug the whole creation.
Want to shout out, "Lord, O,
Glory halleluiah!"
Want to open up, drink in
Manna of salvation, O
The Lord has done great things!

He restored the fortunes of Zion
Praise, praise the Lord—
Hear, hear His Word—
He brings forth the joy from the crying.
We are glad indeed!

Chorus

He and we are one in the Spirit
Praise, praise the Lord—
Hear, hear his word—
Grace comes to judgment for those who fear it—
We are glad indeed!

Chorus

(Bridge) Our mouths are filled with laughter
And our tongues with shouts of joy. [13]

He commanded His law to Jacob
Praise, praise the Lord—
Hear, hear His Word—
His testimony to our fathers—
The Lord has done great things!

Chorus

He lets the children know his works
Praise, praise the Lord—
Hear, hear His Word—

---

[13] This sentence is a paraphrase of Psalm 126:2: "Then was our mouth filled with laughter, and our tongue with singing: then said they among the heathen, The Lord hath done great things for them."

That we might not forget His words.
The Lord has done great things!

Chorus

And children grow, and are blessed with children.
Praise, praise the Lord—
Hear, hear his word—
He gives us strength and patient wisdom!
The Lord has done great things!

*I wrote this on March 30, 1991. Oddly, I remember the
circumstances well. I say "oddly" because often , working to ready these
poems for being part of L/L Research's digital world for seekers to
explore, I find I do not even recall writing an older poem until I
reread it! But writing this one was part of a very intense experience.*

*It was a time of enormous physical challenge in my life and I was
awake during most nights. This night at about 3:00 a.m. I slipped
into an altered state where I was in the light, and could simply see the
perfection of all things. It is a lovely place to be! The feelings were free
in me, and my love of the Creator and for Jesus in particular was
unbounded. I got happier and happier! And then these words came
pouring through, and I was scribbling as fast as I could just to get
them down.*

*I am most grateful for such transmissions! They are not great poems,
but heartfelt and sometimes we don't need great words, just the words
that speak to us right then.*

Like the Rain

The waking sun calls me, Lord, to prayer with You,
The branches touching sky with glowing fingers.
The rosy pale of dawn
Light the bed I lie upon,
My will is Yours. Tell me what I should do.

(Chorus) Like the rain coming down
So your Spirit comes to me, O Lord.
Like the cool, sweet rain on the new-turned earth
So my soul is open to Your Word.

Solomon forsook You, Lord, in the heat of his life's day.
Your statutes and your ways are sometimes shadowed.
In this busy time of noon, Lord, I pray You light me soon.
Like David, I, Thy servant need to see.

Chorus

At eventide, O Lord, my God, in Thee do I take refuge.
Lord, let me see the errors made this day.
To your feast I am a guest. I pray let me be well dressed,
That I may drift to sleep ready to see you.

Chorus

This poem was written on May 14, 1982. It has the marks of Bible Study and probably the scripture Mick and I had read that morning inspired the thoughts that turned into these words.

Little Cottage by the Sea

I have tiny cabin in the mountains.
I have a little cottage by the sea.
The sea is lover to me in the summertime—
I go there often in my dreams.

(Chorus) I skip over water; I dance over sea,
And all the birds in the air couldn't catch me.[14]

(Bridge) "I will lift mine eyes unto the hills
Whence cometh my help."[15]

Getting to my cottage isn't easy.
Living life awake can make you cry.
The land is lover to me in the wintertime,
Caressing into silence my loud, "Why?"

Chorus

Beloved, oh, Beloved, are you there now?
At the mountain cottage you shall be.
Pine and oak cathedral, and the large view,
And the dream that is turning into me.

Bridge

Chorus

I wrote this at Pawley's Island, South Carolina while Mick and I
were on vacation there on August 24, 1985. How I loved that little
haven! The place was not built up with modern condominia, but very
au naturel, beach shacks coexisting in supreme comfort with small,
large, humble and grand homes. The nearby shore boasted many
wonderful restaurants and a women's clothing store that had the best
sale of the year in late summer, when the prices were cheapest. That's
when we always went!

---

[14] These words are believed to have been first published in 1797 in
"Newest Christmas Box."

[15] Psalm 121:1 is the text of this bridge.

Lord, I Feel Your Arms Around Me

Lord, I feel your arms around me
And I know that naught can harm me.
As I bide within Thy grace,

Cradling gently, Thou dost hold me.
Stunned and joyful, I behold Thee:
Unseen mystery, blessed embrace.

(Bridge) Jesus, Thou art my soul's lover.
In Thine agony, my sins You cover.

If I take the wings of morning—
If in farthest parts I'm bourning
Still your hands will be in mine

If I feel by darkness bounded.
If to grave my heart is hounded.
Still Thy light in me shall shine.

Jesus, call me to remembrance
Of Thy arms midst life's encumbrance
Ever present Source and End

As I feel Your arms around me
Help me to return and hold Thee
As in Thee my life I spend.

I wrote this down on January 25, 1993. I was recovering from rehabilitation after major colon surgery in 1992, and had just started the Calvary (Episcopal Church, Louisville, Kentucky) Intercessory Prayer Group, which I led for 23 years before giving it up when I changed parishes due to failing health.

The manuscript shows clearly the fact that the poem was flowing through me, not from me, as it is very hastily written on the back of some Intercessory Prayer stationery. I must have been writing prayer notes when inspiration hit!

Love Was Born Today

Thank you, Lord, for giving me this day.
The snowfall filled my soul
And freshened my whole being
More than words can say.

(Chorus) Love was born today!
Every time I pray
I sing of Christmas Day.

Thank you, Lord, for giving me my friends.
The best are family.
We make each other happy
More than we can comprehend.

Chorus

Abba, Lord, I thank You for Your Son.
For giving Chris to Earth
now all good souls have worth
while ages run.

(Bridge) Jesus
In us!
Blessed Christmas Day!

Chorus

This sentimental poem was written on January 14, 1992, during the time I was writing poems for my brother, Tommy. He did not put this one to a tune, however.

Morning Song

I want to linger longer with the Lord.
My arm, be limber, strong to do His Word.
It's a dizzy, dizzy world
And a busy, busy day.
But I will linger longer with my Lord today.

(Chorus) Just ask Jesus.
Please ask Jesus.

What is the matter, Mister, to make you frown?
And what fell on you, Sister, to bring you down?
Will you go the heart's way?
Alone, it's only part-way?
Just ask Jesus. He'll ease us on the Way.

Chorus

When I get up on Monday, my feet are made of lead.
And all I can think about is how to get back to bed!
Then it's eat and shower,
Dressed and gone in half an hour—
Think I'll linger on the way with my Lord today.

Chorus

I woke up with these words pouring through me on September 18, 1987. It made me so happy to linger a little longer while I scrounged some paper and wrote them down. I was in the middle of a difficult, uncomfortable period in my life, physically speaking, but somehow my inner mood seldom reflects the purely physical, for which I give great thanks.

My Hand to You

Lord, I'm lonely tonight.
The path I walk is not a rest.
I wander, weary, unrequited,
Seeking my "personal best".

(Chorus) I reach out my hand to You. Jesus, You make it so easy.
You see me through, Your hand in mine—
Air when I'm feeling wheezy,
Windbreak when it is breezy,
Oh, peace sublime— Your hand in mine.

Lord, my cowboy is away.
His Avalon shows him his God.
I wistfully wish that he wanted to stay
But sometimes, he must be abroad.

Chorus

Lord, remembering's hard.
Distraction's in all that we see.
If I see you, it's through the bars
Of the prison that I've made for me.

Chorus

Lord, teach me to love.
Beloved Spirit, help me to learn
To pierce the bars; to focus above;
To worship, to praise and discern.

Chorus

I wrote this on May 31, 1991; during the time I was down with several different illnesses at once and could not sit up. I spent day and night on a hospital bed, and Mick cared for me almost completely. Once a week he took a couple of days and a night for himself, retreating on Avalon's wild acres and recovering his equilibrium. Selfishly, I missed him all too much!

Night Song

(Chorus) Tonight the busy world lies hushed and still.
Tomorrow, Father, bend me to Thy will

It's been a good day, Lord. I sold a thousand cases!
It's been fine day, Lord—I won twice at the races.
And the party was so fine, all the best of food and wine.
What a race I've run since the first light of the sun.

Chorus

It's been a hard day, Lord—I took a bath in futures.
It's been a rough one, Lord—my soul is full of sutures.
And the surgeons of the soul, they seldom leave one whole.
What a race I've run since the first light of the sun.

Chorus

It's been my own day, Lord—full of my small thinking.
I have a hard head, Lord, harder than your linking
And my mind is such a stone that rolls firmly on its own.
What a selfish race I've run since the first light of the sun.

Chorus

I cannot recall writing this poem. It is dated April 24, 1986. "Are You Running with Me Jesus?" was a prayer I enjoyed, written by a priest and friend, Father Ken Thompson, and my poem grew up around the question his prayer posed in my own mind. What a blessing Father Ken has been in my life! His generosity and good advice have often aided me through the decades. I lost track of Father Ken when I left the congregation of Calvary Church for St. Luke's, but then he began to work at St. Luke's after the turn of the century, so I have continued to appreciate him.

O Spirit, Come!

He formed us from the womb to be his servants.
He hid us in the shadow of his hand.
He gave us as a light to all the nations,
That coastland, hill and plain hear his command.

(Chorus) O Spirit, come! O Spirit, speak!
Through us may God's bright glory shine!
O holy One of Israel,
Send forth through us Thy love divine.

He gives us words with wings to call the peoples.
He gives us speech to sting the sinners' pride.
He urges us to toil though we prevail not.
Our perfect place is at our Master's side.

Chorus

When Kings and Princes find his great salvation,
The earth shall rise as one to speak His praise
The Holy One of Israel has chosen
That all shall be His people all our days.

Chorus

This was written on January 18, 1987. I think it must be a close match to a psalm I was struck by during a Sunday service there, although I am not sure which one.

Only the True Vine Giveth Life

Once a sweet vine, a flowing vine
Grew around my lilac trees
And its beauty me did blind.
But it was strangling my lilac trees.

(Chorus) In the sweep of my side yard grow lilac trees.
I sit me down beneath their shade.
I discard my worries and let my mind be.
The stress and strain just go away.

Chorus

Only the true vine giveth life
And I'll drink the fruit of that vine in the Kingdom
But the false vine causes death and strife
So, abide in me, Lord. Prune me in your wisdom

Chorus

In the daytime, when the sun is high
I will labor at many things
And my heart brings me such a foolish pride
As I strive for nothing but wind

Chorus

Father, listen to my humble prayer
As I sit beneath my lilac trees.
Teach me love so passing fair
As I strip the vines away from me.

(Coda) Why do we let our lives get so complicated?
The Father is simplicity.
Stop my parade, for peace is indicated.
O Jesus, come to me.

Chorus

I imagine I wrote this during the mid-nineties, when I was studying with the Calvary Church bible class on Tuesdays and readying the altar for Holy Eucharist.

Quietly, Ye Workers of the Lord

(Chorus) Quietly, ye workers of the Lord,
In confidence, go forth to do His bidding.
You never know just what the day will bring.
The Spirit offers all that may be fitting.

Have you known of Hiram, a workingman of Tyre?
He came to work for Solomon, a-smelting in the fire.
The tribe of Naphtali could stand and view the house of Solomon
And know that its own humble son did build the house of
Solomon.

Chorus

Have you known of Jesus, a man from Galilee?
His love has lifted up so many sinners such as me.
He came to toil, a shepherd strong, attending to His sheep.
And when His hour came, He did pray, "Thy will is good for me."

Chorus

Now it is the moment when you may open wide
Your hand, and cast your grain of wheat upon the countryside.
What gifts are these? O watch and pray, And let the seedlings die
away
For soon the earth will know your fruit if you but give in faith
today.

*Clearly, I wrote this during the Bible Study Tuesdays period in the
mid-nineties. It was a very intense time of study and learning for me,
for I came early each week to set the table of the altar for Communion
after the Bible Study was done. Then I stayed after we had finished in
the sanctuary to clear and clean the altar and make it ready for the
next service.*

*I had time both before and after the study to muse in silent service,
touching most humbly the sacred chalice, paten and all the rest of the
silver and linens—first for the service to come, and then when we were
finished with that. The service itself always moves me, and of course I
would be thinking about the Holy Scripture I'd studied that day. It
made me more focused on bible-Christianity than I usually am.*

I generally came with JoAn Shuler, a fellow parishioner who was a dear, dear friend for many years. She has passed into larger life.

Singing up to Heaven from the Cross

Daybreak—
One branch stirs with hidden anthem.
Heartbreak.
The carpenter is far from Bethlehem
Nearer to the sky
Is the cross.
Evermore shall I
Count this loss.

(Chorus) You gave your life for me.
I give mine back to You, my Heart.
Just for today let me be
Yours in every part,
Doer of your will,
Bearer of your joy,
Singing up to heaven from the cross.

Day stirs.
Footsteps fall in quiet houses.
Laughter,
Kitchen bright with morning's promises,
Family at grace
Holding hands,
Sleepy, loving faces
Of my life's friends.

Chorus

Sun high.
Hammer pounds upon the lumber
Birds fly
By. I cannot count the number.
Restful is the run
You inspire.
Single as the sun
Is my desire.

Chorus

This poem is dated simply "Lent, 1984". I remember joining in a Quiet Day at Calvary, and writing this after a long period of contemplation upon the crucifixion of Jesus the Christ.

Sinner's Song

If I am soil and You the plow, then I must not be hard.
If I receive the seed you sow, with ruts I'll first be marred.
I've so many weeds to give away! Why do I want to keep them?
Tares of pain and loss of faith—why do You wish to receive them?

(Chorus) Lord, have mercy on me, a sinner
Christ, have mercy on me, a sinner
Lord, have mercy on me, a sinner.

Christe eleison.
Kyrie eleison.

I was not enough alone. All my will fell short.
All my teeth and hair and bone were dust at Lazarus' port.
I was not enough with another, though Your praise I offered.
Though I loved 'til day was through, it did not fill Your coffers.

Chorus

(Bridge) Why did He have to suffer?
Why did He have to fear?
He was better and wiser and tougher—
Why did He die, while I'm still here?

I live in knots of confusion. My sins are like a hide
Staked with the earth of illusion, which now I can scarcely abide.
Lord, let my surface meniscus break; pour me out like sand.
If dust and dirt doubt that You're with us, unbelief never weakens
Your hand.

(Bridge) Why am I still living
When my faith was unavailing?
Thanks for this day of giving.
Teach me to trust through my failings.

Chorus

*I wrote this on March 7, 1984, but these would be my sentiments any
time from the womb onward! I do not recall a human moment
wherein I have been satisfied with my devotion to Jesus. I know there
is always more I could give, if I could find it!*

Sketches of the Crucifixion

I

The sun came up on a misty fence
And the cows bent their heads to chew more daisies.
An early pale butterfly climbed a tree,
And climbed, and fluttered, and fell to the burnt grass.
The hills ran at fog towards the higher left,
Spilling towards the right, downhill,
The fog. One eagle fled the morning star.

II

Sixteen-year-old Ella Duncan slammed the door.
Behind her, indignantly, wearily;
Stalked to the corner with the speed of rebellion;
Met David Junior, who had an underslung jaw,
Twitched and wore a twisted undershirt.
As she passed him, jostling him aside,
He leered and said, "I love you."

III

The schooner's carpenter was ending the repairs
On the mast. His hands were rope-sore as he
Mounted the rigging. He used them to live by.
As He stretched to reach a nail, he stopped, and tensed,
And quietly dropped into the choppy sea.
The gulping fish exchanged blank nods to see
Him drink the sea as if it gave him life.

*I wrote this while I was in college, attempting to make the poem's
images draw the sacred cross, first one way, and then another. It was
probably 1963 when this came to me. It can fairly be said that Jesus
and His Passion are ever on my mind.*

Son of Simon

(Simon's son was Judas Iscariot)

I looked down at my feet, white islands in the rain.
Hear the jackals feed? Never see them come.
Walking in the rain, waiting for the sun
To come out again, son of Simon

(Chorus) We all lose our way. We all do our best.
Son of Simon—stay; stay your hand, at last.

Our computer eyes never see us do it.
No one ever buys 'til he's driven to it.
I can sit and wait. I can judge and spell,
But my bus is driven by a child from hell.

Chorus

*I wrote this song on May 24, 1984. I had learned that Judas simply
wanted Jesus to be an earthly king and wrest control of Israel back
from Rome. When the mind is biased by fear, we can feel it is only
right to defend oneself, one's people and one's land. Judas could not
hear Jesus, calm statement: "Get thee behind me, Satan. My kingdom
is not of this world."*

True Vine

In my door yard grows a lilac tree
And I sat me down beneath its shade.
I just discard all my worries;
All my fears just fade away.

(Chorus) Only the true vine giveth life
And I'll drink the fruit of that vine in the Kingdom.
But the false vine causes death and strife
So abide in me, Lord, prune me with your wisdom.

Once a sweet vine, a flowering vine
Grow around my lilac tree,
And its beauty blinded me,
But it was strangling my lilac tree.

Chorus

In the daytime, when the sun is high,
I will labor at many things,
And my heart bring me such a foolish pride
As I strive for nothing but wind.

Chorus

(Bridge) Why do we let our lives get so confused?
The Father is simplicity.
Father, stop my big parade.
Oh, Lord Jesus, come to me.

Father, listen to my humble prayer
As I sit beneath my lilac trees:
As I took the vine from its branches fair,
Strip the false vines away from me.

Chorus

When Don, Mick and I were living on Watterson Trail on September 1, 1980, where almost all of the Ra sessions were held, I realized that a large, lovely lilac tree near the driveway was being killed by a pernicious vine. I worked for days at removing the vine.

Upon the Path

Upon the path I wend my way.
Alleluia!
In caverns close I stop to pray.
Alleluia!
My mind is fixed on Him always
Through space and time and length of days.
Alleluia!

At last the citadel is gained.
Alleluia!
And not without the price of pain.
Alleluia!
For without effort, without strain,
The soul seeks Jesus' cross in vain.
Alleluia!

O joy! To sit within the tower!
Alleluia!
To gaze at Heaven by the hour.
Alleluia!
O Jesus, take my heart to scour.
Cleanse my soul with Thy great power.
Alleluia!

In this wondrous room of prayer,
Alleluia—
Where at last we seek no more.
Alleluia!
All in all is Christ most fair!
In my heart He nestles there.
Alleluia!

I do not recall when I wrote this. I'd guess it as in the 1970s. These sentiments have been mine for a lifetime.

Wait for the Lord

It's so easy to throw it all away!
Squeeze a Christian, and out comes the regulation guy.
When the workers at the office have their say
We are liable to give it back, eye for eye!

(Chorus) But we need to pull back and we need to think long.
It is time to wait upon the Lord.
It's time for prayer and time for song.
It is time to wait and watch for the Lord.

Let our lamps be lit, however late,
Though it's hard to do in this confusion.
It's so easy to say all the right-sounding words,
Quote the Bible in eloquent profusion.

Chorus

It's difficult to live the Word,
It's often hard to hear the Spirit's voice.
It's not just for you that I'm playing these chords.
In the end, I am singing my Choice.

(Bridge) "Let your loving kindness be upon us, Lord
As we have put our trust in you.".[16]

It's so easy to bury our gold
Because we do not want to risk loss.
But the talents we have are on loan, not sold,
And one day we'll fully be accountable to the boss.

Chorus

I wrote this in May of 1982, reflecting upon Father Ben Sander's sermon on Sunday. He was a marvelous man of God and an astute and excellent preacher, as well as a much appreciated shepherd of souls.

---

[16] I was pondering Psalm 37-7, which in the King James Version of the Bible reads "Rest in the Lord and wait patiently for Him: fret not thyself because of him who prospereth in his way, because of the man who bringeth wicked devices to pass."

The Watches of the Night

Through the watches of the night, I wait for Thee.
While the moonlight falls like snow
And the shadows come and go,
I crouch small within my soul and think to flee.
Where to travel from the devil?
Faults within at every level.
And I'm deathly tired of focusing on me.

(Chorus) So Come! Let us walk in the light of the Lord!
Let us seek the boon of quietness and peace.
Come! Let's be glad in the City of the Lord.
And praise shall cause our inner dark to cease.

Through the watches of the night, I gaze unblinking,
While my clock, the thief of sleep,
Ticking, mocks the silence deep.
Reclining with my sins, I try not thinking,
But regrets mount to the stars,
And self-judgment builds the bars
Of the prison within which my soul lies shrinking.

Chorus

Through the watches of the night my heart's in prayer.
Since I find myself awake,
I will this advantage take
For salvation nears, and Jesus comes, most fair!
If He does not come tonight,
Yet to watch and pray is right,
And, in Jesus' name, I let go all my care.

Chorus

I wrote this on December 9, 1986. During the late seventies and all of the eighties and nineties I had a chronic problem with sleeplessness. Pain would not let my consciousness sink down into healthy rest. Many times I watched television or read a book. At other times I gave myself up to reflection and let the night pass as it would. I wrote this during one of those contemplative night times when I was awake till the dawning.

We Are Glad Indeed

(Chorus) I want to jump up, reach out, and hug the whole
creation.
Want to shout out Lord, O, glory halleluiah!
Want to open, drink in manna of salvation!
O, the Lord has done great things!

He restored the fortunes of Zion!
Praise, praise the Lord! Hear, hear his word!
He brings forth the joy from the crying.
We are glad indeed!

Chorus

He and we are one in the Spirit
Praise, praise the Lord! Hear, hear his Word!
Grace comes to judgment for those who fear it—
We are glad indeed!

Chorus

He commanded His law to Jacob
Praise, praise the Lord! Hear, hear his word!
His testimony to our father—
The Lord has done great things!

(Bridge) Our mouths are filled with laughter
And our tongues with shouts of joy.

Chorus

He lets His children know His works.
Praise, praise the Lord! Hear, hear his word!
That we might not forget his words.
The Lord has done great things!

Chorus

And children grow, and are blessed with children
Praise, praise the Lord! Hear, hear his word!
He gives us strength and wisdom!
The Lord has done great things

Chorus

I wrote this somewhere around 1980. Tommy and I never developed the song for our singing.

We Are Pilgrims

No one knows the depth of a pilgrim's sorrow.
No one sees the dreams hid till tomorrow.
You can't hear me crying. I can't feel your pain.
We could all by lying. We could be insane.
No one knows another's sorrow.

(Chorus) We are pilgrims on the King's Highway.
Each walking by himself; each goal the same.
The goal is love, the grail, redemption
Hearts raised high to find salvation.
To human eyes, we're all alone
But in the Lord we all are one.

Far ahead, I see other pilgrims walking,
By the road, the sore-footed talking
Trying to gain strength from each other's courage,
Letting go of every umbrage.
Weary, hopeful pilgrims walking.

Chorus

If we are truly one, let us embrace now.
Christian, Muslim, Buddhist, Jew, we race now
To hold each other tightly, to wish each other well.
Each of us is right; each story good to tell.
We are one, let's all embrace now.

Chorus

Can we save our Earth from war's disaster?
Can we join in thanks, in praise and laughter?
No one knows the truth; no one can explain
Why we keep causing each other so much pain.
Only faith can bring us pilgrims home.

Chorus

(Coda) Behind all the shadows lies the One God.
Behind all the stories dwells the One Love.
Though separated by opinion,
When speech is ended we are all One.

I have no memory of writing this poem, but a marginal note dates it February 17, 1991.

Weeping Mary

Weeping Mary, tell me why you cry?
Sweetest Magdalene, please dry your eye.
"You weren't there.
You never knew Him.
He was my everything.
Now He is gone."

Weeping Mary, tell me who am I?
Sweetest Magdalene, please lift your eyes.
Suddenly
You come before me.
Your robes are dazzling!
But Rabbi is gone.

(Bridge) Hand on the telephone, hugging your sorrow,
There is no woe that won't leave you tomorrow
Weeping Mary, hold on through the night,
Sweetest Magdalene, 'til morning's light.

Weeping Mary, why seek Life in graves?
Sweetest Magdalene, why would He stay?
My bones shake
With grief and confusion
Don't know who you are.
But where is my Lord?

Weeping Mary, all the world's a grave
Sweetest Magdalene, He lives to save.

I wrote this during a very difficult season of suffering, at Easter of 1984, when Don was seemingly gone and replaced by a stranger with navy eyes who looked at me longingly but could not be in my presence without doing violence to himself. That ended in the most incredible tragedy of my life at his police-forced suicide on November 7.

And I was so ill. It was as if I wanted to go after him into death. My gall bladder was removed in 1986. The other, worse, problem with my colon was solved through major surgery removing half the transverse colon in January 1992.

What Seek Ye?

What seek ye, seek ye, seek ye, stranger from afar?
I seek a distant, glorious star.

Why seekest thee one tiny child?
I seek a love so pure and mild

Why seek thee strife and pain and danger?
A seeker is the eternal stranger.

Oh, seeker, will your trip e'er end?
Those who seek, they shall be fed.

Glory to God n the highest
Peace on earth, that all may rest.

Do you seek the star?
Yes, the star above.
Do you seek the child?
Yes, the child of love.
Do you seek the cries?
Yes the cries of strife.
Do you seek the bread?
Yes, the bread of life.

I wrote this for The Journey, *which is a story-with-songs, where I wrote the story and songs and Tommy put the songs to music. We did this is the late eighties. The story is about the journey of the Magi. When I get to that point I will try to complete this song and type in the surrounding story as well.*

Where Is the Mercy?

(Chorus) "Eli, Eli lama sabachtani!
You have forsaken me!"
Where is the mercy?
Sometimes it's hard to trust in Thee.

It's hard to see my friend locking his chain,
Turning the key shut once again,
Does he need it? Can he use it?
Freedom's right within his grasp!
All he needs to do is ask.
Does he fear it? He's so near it—
(But he says)

Chorus

(Bridge) "*Those who are planted in the house of the Lord*
Shall flourish, shall find nourishment, in the courts of our God!"[17]

I do it myself, see a cloudy sky,
And drink up all the shadows bye and bye.
Do I need it? Can I use it?
Challenges will run me down,
And by myself, I fall flat on the ground
Do I fear Him when I'm so near Him?
(But I say)

Chorus

Maybe one day before I'm gray
I'll have it figured out what it means to pray.
Oh I need it. I can use it!
Sad, sick, hungry, yes, the world is flawed,
But when I am rooted in the living Lord,
There is feeling. There's healing.
(And I still ask)

Chorus

Bridge

---

[17] This is a quotation from Psalm 92:14.

I wrote, according to a marginal note, in 1980 or 1981. This was right at the beginning of the Ra contact.

Will You Let Me?

She was afraid of fire!
She had to jump from a second-story window frame
Into the net.
Was so hot and shot through with tongues of flame!
She wasn't ready yet.

(Chorus) Oh, I'm reaching out to you, my family in Christ
Won't you reach back to me? You won't have to do it twice.
We're all children of the Lord, one great family.
I'm reaching out to touch you. Will you let me?

He was terrified of love!
He felt the flame that made him whole.
He knew it was good.
Jesus had answered the questions inside,
But he couldn't decide

Chorus

(Bridge) Unfurl our wings
Till our hearts start to sing!

We're afraid of faith!
We have so much to let go before we cast off
Into the sea
Then the waters of peace wash the dust of this world.
Still, we reckon the fee

Chorus

*I wrote this on July 17, 1980, the summer before the Ra contact
began, while we were moving to Watterson Trail. Perhaps it presaged
the Ra contact, confessing my doubts, ahead of time, that I was ready
or worthy of such an honor. I certainly felt under-prepared during the
contact many times as my body failed. But I became very sure as I saw
Don's joy in this conversation with those of Ra, and lived only to do
another session.*

The Word

"And the word of the Lord was as rare in those days,"
Thus Samuel told the tale,
"As if the night sky were covered with haze
And inner vision failed"
But the Lamp of God had not yet dimmed
And Eli's eyes were clear.
Eli, old, with palsied limb,
You knew the Word so dear.

(Chorus) Why don't we listen?
The Word is all about us,
Within us and without us?
Let our hearts be opened,
That we never miss His sound,
"And let none of His words fall to the ground"

"For this people's heart has grown dull", said Isaiah
"And their eyes they have closed"
Rare, so rare, are the prayers to pray;
Buried deep, our souls,
But blessed still are the eyes that do see
And ears that still do hear
Understanding shall surely come to be
And joy dry seekers' tears

Chorus

There are always a few who seek to plant His seeds;
They sprout a hundredfold.
There have always been many who never feel the need
To use the seed of gold.
Even we who cry, "Here am I, Lord, Here!"
Are full of rocky ground
But, together, let us to use our eyes
And hear the Spirit's sound.

Chorus

I wrote this on January 20, 1982. To read the Bible is to catch the
rhythms of a more formal and beautiful version of the English

language and for that reason I would guess I wrote this while pondering a reading I'd experienced one Sunday from the old Testament.

Ye Workers of the Lord

(Chorus) Quietly, ye workers of the Lord,
In confidence go forth to do His bidding.
Ye know not what the day will bring,
The Spirit offers all that may be fitting.

Have you known of Hiram, a workingman of Tyre?
He came to work for Solomon a-smelting in the fire.
The tribe of Naphtali could stand and view the house of Solomon
And know that their own humble son did build the house of
Solomon

Chorus

Have you known of Jesus, a man from Galilee?
He came to toil, a shepherd strong, a-tending to His sheep.
All Earth's folk were taught His Name, and when His hour did
came, He prayed
"O, Father, glorify Thy name!" And then the voice from heaven
rang.

Chorus

Now it is the moment when you may open wide
Your hand, and cast your grain of wheat upon the countryside.
What gifts, are these? O watch and pray, and let the seedlings lie.
Know your fruit will come if you but give in faith today.

Chorus

*I wrote this in 1992, when I began studying the Bible each Tuesday
at Calvary.*

You Really Move Me!

You're the guy on Ararat that sent out the dove,
I think the olive branch has a meaning—
You're the guy sent Moses down that fire from above—
I don't know your home town, but I hear you speaking.

(Chorus) You really move me!
Please use me.
You really blow me away!

It's so easy thinking that we're on to something great,
But lots of times we're let down in the end.
It's so hard to accept when we're too early or too late.
It's lovely just to take what you send.

Chorus

How did Joshua know when to blow his horn?
How did Jesus know to walk the sea?
How much do our infants know when they are barely born?
The spirit is a mystery to me.

(Bridge) I love it! It thrills me—
Spirit, always take me!
Never let me drift far from Thee.

Chorus

*I wrote this on December 22, 1980. The day before Jim McCarty
arrived at Watterson Trail to join Don and me at L/L Research. I am
sure that my mood was ebullient because of his return, but as always,
my mind was on Jesus, my Beloved. It shows my eternally naïve,
childlike enthusiasm for the Lord. Perhaps it also expresses my
happiness at Jim's return to us.*

Manufactured by
Amazon.ca
Bolton, ON